Nina Sadur

One of Russia's most eminent dramatists, whose plays
have been staged widely in her native country and abroad,
Nina Sadur is less known as a prose writer, although her
stories and short novels have been published in most
major Russian literary journals.

Born in 1950 in Novosibirsk, Nina Sadur came to
Moscow in 1977, where she lives to this day. She gradu-
ated from the city's Gorky Institute of Literature in 1983.

The stories and novella *The South* collected in this
volume were written in the early years of the 1990's.
Sadur's richly-textured, dramatic prose is distinctive in
contemporary Russian literature for its combination of
colloquial language and rhythms with a complex, poetic
style, which transforms seemingly everyday locations and
events into part of an emotionally-charged private world.

Cathy Porter

Cathy Porter is a writer and reviewer who has specialised
for more than two decades in translations from Russian;
she now also translates from Czech. The author of origi-
nal biographies of Russian writers Alexandra Kollontai
and Larisa Reisner, her wide range of translation has
encompassed fiction, drama, travel and history, including
the diaries of Sofia Tolstoy. She translated and adapted
Nina Sadur's radio play, *Star-Boy*, for BBC Radio broad-
cast in 1996. Cathy Porter lives in London.

Witch's Tears

and Other Stories

By Nina Sadur

Translated from the Russian by Cathy Porter

Harbord Publishing

Published by Harbord Publishing Limited
58 Harbord Street, London SW6 6PJ.

First published in Russian as *Vedminy Slezki*, Glagol Publishing, Moscow, 1994
© Nina Sadur, 1997
Translation © Cathy Porter, 1997
The moral rights of the author and translator have been asserted.

British Library Cataloguing in Publication data.
A CIP record for this book is available from the British Library.

Printed in England by Hartnolls Limited, Bodmin, Cornwall.

ISBN 1 899414 15 0

Witch's Tears	7
Rings	14
Cold	22
Flowering	28
Unrequited Love	32
Closer to Rest	35
Star-Boy	45
Diamonds and Irons	65
The Wind from the Suburbs	74
The South	99

Witch's Tears

Quietly, as though breathing, the boards of the pavement creaked. In Ordynsk they still had the old pavements, the wooden ones. Go down Sibirsk Street to the newspaper kiosk, they said, then turn left towards "their" houses, and the green one was the witch's.

She had brought fifteen roubles and his photograph, taken long before he had met her. It showed a very young soldier – he was still soft and curly, with a bright grin on his downy lips.

She had been given the witch's address by her friend Galya, in secret of course. Galya told her to go late in the evening, near night-time, and to take money.

The pavement ended unexpectedly, and Nadya stepped on to bare earth. In the distance, the kiosk loomed up. Reaching it she turned left, into a row of wooden houses drowning in a dark thicket of cherry trees and maples. She walked down the dark street, past the watchful, silent houses in which they had told her lived many Tartars. They refused to let their beautiful daughters marry Russians. Blood had flowed here not long ago.

She thought she would be unable to find the green house in the dark, but she found it at once – she knew it was green even though it was as black as the rest of the street.

She knocked. She knocked again. And again.

Someone sighed. She started knocking continuously, trembling all over and hugging to her left shoulder the flat white bag with the fifteen roubles and the photograph.

In the yard was a shed. In the shed lived a pig. It was the pig sighing. "It's probably bewitched," the girl thought, hearing it grunt. "I expect the witch is out seeing friends," she decided as still no one opened the door.

Just as she had given up and was about to leave, the door quietly opened a crack, wafting the smell of roasted onion over her, and in the dim light of the crack she saw the witch.

The witch did not speak, just gave her a brief look, and leaving the door slightly open, she turned her back on the girl and walked into the room.

There was nothing for it but to go in uninvited. Covering her heart with her bag the girl stepped over the threshold and the door slammed shut after her, as though it were angry.

"Must be the draft," thought Nadya, taking courage from the normal, habitable room which met her eyes. Walking to the table in the middle, laid with a nice clean cloth, she stood looking around for the old woman.

At that moment something quivered in her hand, became warm, breathed fearfully, pulled away and flapped its wings in her face.

"My bag!" shrieked Nadya, grabbing for the white dove into which the mischievous witch had turned her bag.

She heard laughter behind her back, and she laughed too – the dove was so sweet, with its soft bulging wings and the curly crest on its small round head.

"Sit down, girl," said the witch, pointing to a Viennese table and chair.

The girl sat down and looked at the witch, who turned out to be just an old woman in a strange, sad, bright-coloured linen dress with big pockets and a long skirt falling down in sad, tired folds.

The dove was hopping around the table, not at all afraid of them, and Nadya could see that its breast was pulsating and contracting – just like a real heart, there was no doubting it. What was even more suspicious, though she didn't understand why and it didn't really alarm her, was the little crimson spot at its centre. The spot was hard and bulging, like the gem on a medallion, and when the light of the lamp shone on it, it threw back fine rays.

The witch strode around the room, apparently deep in thought and not noticing Nadya. Unwillingly tearing her bewitched eyes from the dove, Nadya looked at her. Apart from her somewhat surprising dress, she wore white socks and cheap but festively bright oilskin sandals with wide straps. Her face was pale, very old and almost flat, like a picture. Her whole body was tall, thin and flat, as though cut out of cardboard.

The witch paced the room silently, intensely, not looking at Nadya and not asking her anything. Nadya sat meek and afraid, staring at the old woman and also saying nothing.

The yellow curtain at the window twitched. The window was not closed, just covered by the curtain. "Perhaps it's just stirring in the wind," thought Nadya, tensing. But no, out there behind the curtain things were swarming, stirring, pushing, whimpering. Flowers – heavy, white-stemmed clusters of flowers – pushed through the window babbling plaintively, thrusting their stubborn little foreheads through the curtain and into the room.

"Be off!" shouted the witch, stamping her foot and waving her arms at them, at which the flowers squeaked and disappeared.

They weren't flowers though, they were the round, bright heads of babies. Trying not to die of fright, the girl pressed her knees tightly together, squeezed them with her fists and stuck out her chin. "I'm here for Vitka, for a curse on my soldier," she repeated to herself, "quick, tell her now, give her the money, quick..."

She turned her head to the witch and opened her mouth.

"Be quiet," the witch waved her arm at her. A large, freckled arm.

Then something terrible happened. Nadya knew it was happening, and where it was happening – on the table – and that if she looked, her heart would be unable to endure it and would burst. But as always in life, she couldn't not look; what destroys us, attracts us. And her look, crazed and wandering, drew her to the circle of light on the table-cloth, where the dove stood rooted to the spot, its head tipped to one side, its curly white crest looking like plaster-of-Paris, or shampoo suds in a child's hair when you stand it in front of the mirror to stick it up into weird shapes. The dove's eyes, enveloped in a thin film, were sleeping, unaware of what was happening to her. She felt nothing, no fear, but her beak was growing, lengthening, curling, bending to her golden heart, which grew cold in fearful anticipation.

"I must not look, I must not look," the girl muttered, opening her eyes wide, fearing and knowing what was about to happen, and knowing *why* too. Fumbling for the heart, the beak pecked lightly at the red gem and drank. Only it wasn't a gem, it was blood encased in a fine membrane. The beak pecked through it and drank, leaving an empty hollow like the setting for a jewel in a ring. At that the heart shuddered and froze, and the dove, having killed herself, fell on the table with wings outspread, her beak short as before and half-open.

The girl's confidence in her plan collapsed, and her body was flooded with weakness, like after an illness. But her spirits remained strong.

"It makes no difference," she said doggedly, "I want a curse on him. He betrayed me, he didn't marry me, I killed my baby. Make a curse on him."

"Get up," said the witch. The girl got up. "You'll do

what I tell you. Say one word and it won't work. Give me the picture."

The girl took her white bag from the table and pulled out the photograph of his face. She glanced at it; how young he looked, her clear-eyed little soldier.

"Does your heart suffer no envy?" asked the witch.

She was about to say it did not, then realised she must say nothing and that the witch had deliberately asked her so that the spell wouldn't work, like that game people play when they're children, about the lady, the besom and the crown. So she said nothing, and let the witch think she suffered from envy rather than pain and despair.

She stood up and held out the photograph to the witch. The witch took it without looking at it, tossed it into a soot-blackened saucepan, then added herbs and water. Suddenly, from out of nowhere, a weak blue flame and a choking smoke appeared from under the saucepan.

The witch stood looking at the saucepan, muttered something, waved her arms and started to yawn – this, they had told Nadya, was the devils coming to her call, her incantation. A little cloud sprang up on one side and in this cloud the form of a little man appeared, staring around him and flapping his arms ridiculously. It was *him*!

Then it was all over. The witch stopped yawning, waved her arm for the last time, everything disappeared, and she carried the saucepan back into the kitchen. Returning, she sat down opposite Nadya and looked through her, pale and half-asleep. The girl rocked on her chair, wondering if the curse was finished and she could go now, but she said nothing, knowing she wasn't to speak.

"Now you must go to the river. Walk backwards, not looking behind you, till I tell you to stop. Then take the stocking off your left leg and a hair from your left temple, and he will be cursed."

So she got up and, accompanied by the witch, she went out into the street, walking backwards to the river, looking neither behind her nor at the witch who advanced upon her with fixed, empty gaze. Anything for him to be cursed! It was scary. They walked on, down the Tatar road where blood had flowed and they didn't let their daughters marry Russians. One light was shining, the next wasn't, one was, the next wasn't... The witch advanced, and she kept walking backwards as the witch had told her, ordered her – so that the witch was pursuing her and she was retreating.

The road ended and behind her back a fresh river breeze sprang up, with the smell of water, silt and diesel. A steamer hooted. There was sand underfoot now. Could she look up? Silently, yes. Above her the stars were shining, twinkling at her as she cursed her lover. Ah, how he had loved her, how gentle and passionate he had been, the words he had whispered to her. And now she was cursing him. Ah, how he had tortured her. What else could she do?

Soon she would stop, take her stocking off her left leg. Vitka's heart would ache, he would sink, wither and die. He had gone with other girls. He wouldn't go with them any more. But when would it be over for her?

The stars quivered restlessly in the sky. Were they sending her a message? Soon now, soon. It was all because of him. All the pain and fear she'd gone through for him. Soon he would be gone. Vanished. Forever. The end.

But then who would she have to suffer for, swear at? No one. The world would be empty, nothing but night.

It wasn't too late, she could still stop, say something. Otherwise she would have no one to suffer for.

Her feet were wet now. Stop, stop, she was cold, she wanted to go home – a glass of milk and honey, sleep, the pillow wet with tears. Now the water was gripping her legs, her stomach, it was freezing her chest. How good it would be to be at home, falling asleep in bed with her little kitten Murka, watching through sleepy eyelids the geranium on the window. In the morning it would be off to work, then the cinema...

The water was in her throat now. One should never kill anyone!

"Hey, Granny, I...!" Gulp.

The sound of cheerful music could be heard from the steamer, and bright lights sailed past. From them you could see an old woman in white standing on the shore with uplifted face and drooping, lifeless arms.

She wandered slowly back, put on the light in her bare room, tidied up and put the chair back in its place. Then she sat by the window, waiting.

Soon there was a groan outside, and through the window slipped an apparition in a shirt, soaking wet, with water dripping off her.

Falling on her knees, the apparition stretched out her pale arms to the old woman. "You have destroyed me! Not him, me! Make the curse! And make it for him!"

"Go back, your place is there, in the river," said the witch. "You will be the light of the river, you will fly over the lighthouses, you will steer the ships, frighten the buoy-keepers. That is your place. That is your freedom."

The apparition flew off, and the old woman dried the floor, sat again by the window and waited for nothing. She cried. She felt sorry for the poor girl who was so young, but the soldier slept peacefully, knowing nothing. No one would insult him now.

Kindness is all very well – bright, open, nothing but joy, nothing to be afraid of. But when the suffering turn to evil, who knows what torment this brings when aroused, roaming the earth at the behest of pain and injustice?

Rings

There's something about rings, of course. Like dreams. If dreams reflect one side of our life, rings reflect the other.

Dreams show us pictures, so we understand moments which were just hinted at in life, or which went wrong. Rings silently draw in life without separating the moments, and show themselves only at its most important instances. I could give lots of examples of rings and dreams but I'd get muddled, so instead I'll just take love and friendship.

My best friend is Lyubka Vakheta. She's seventeen, three years younger than me. We live in the same building. She made friends with me in the lift. I was in the eighth year at school, she was in the sixth. She caught up with me and rode down with me in the lift. "You want to go for a walk with me today?" she said. I was a bit surprised by this, coming from a year sixer, but I soon got used to it and now we've grown so alike even our mums can't tell us apart.

My Lyubka has led me astray, I'm always bunking off college now. But now when I look at the kids in my class they all look so straight, while every day seems a holiday with my Lyubka.

She doesn't know a thing. She doesn't even know in which year the war started.

"Twenty million," she says.

"Right," I say, "that's how many was killed."

"So who's President of the United States now?" she asks. "Kennedy?"

"Give me a break," I say. "It's Reagan!"

"Funny," she says, "wonder why I thought it was Kennedy."

She's very pretty, our Lyubka, with sharp little teeth and blue, blue eyes. She's always thinking about drugs, shuddering with emotion and trying not to get thin. She eats so much, I've never seen anyone eat like her. She's bursting out of all her clothes. She comes up, asks me for a sweet and gobbles it up – but that suits me fine because I want to lose weight.

Lyubka really disgraced herself out at the farm, though. She's forever disgracing herself, but she disgraced herself at Black Earth to last a lifetime.

We both fell in love at Black Earth – me with Levan, her with Sasha – but I was more scared for Lyubka because she's so irresponsible. Sasha didn't try anything with me, he was polite and proper as anything, nothing dirty, but he treated Lyubka like a whore. And she was just an innocent virgin. It was disgusting. To start with they got along fine together, he really liked her. But when he found out she was still a virgin he went cold on her, and then she went mad. The boys were staying at the second camp, so one night Lyubka asked some of our lot to go over the fields with her to this other camp. The ones she picked were drunk, and they all dragged over the bumpy field with her in the dark, and when they reached the platform outside the other camp she dumped the drunk ones. Then Sasha said, "I've got thirty minutes for you," and she came back again.

But that's nothing. We were picking water-melons one day and Lyubka found this little ring, all black and trampled-on, with a dirty, watery jewel in the middle. We both laughed, and she put it in her jacket and forgot about it. Only Lyubka could find a ring in the middle of a water-melon field.

So we come back to Moscow, and Lyubka gets ready to give herself to Sasha because she has no alternative – he refuses to be just friends. Her mum starts smoking, her dad hits the tranquillisers, her gran's legs get paralysed.

"Buy me a pair of white knickers, Mum!" Lyubka demands. She can never keep anything to herself.

Her mum's in tears. "Don't think I don't know what you're up to, you silly slag! You'd better find yourself another boy if it's come to that, because he's scum!"

So Lyubka calls him up.

"Hi, Sasha!" she goes.

"How you doing?" he goes.

"Why didn't you call me?"

"Too busy."

"But we got on really well at camp!"

"You promised to do it, but you didn't."

"You knew I was a virgin, it'd be boring for you, I wouldn't know how."

"Do it first, talk later."

"Later you'd ditch me. If you're going to ditch me, I won't do it."

"So don't phone me."

That's how he talks to her. Then I call Sasha and say: "First, I'm telling you not to let Lyubka know I phoned. Second, I want to remind you of the article in the Criminal Code about corruption of minors. Just thought you should know!"

Next time Lyubka phones him he says: "Don't call me again, you don't attract me as a woman."

And all this time the ring is lying there forgotten in her pocket.

Now about Levan. The reason he has that name is that he's from Georgia, and they all have funny names down there. But he's Russian, christened even. Married. And I fell desperately in love with him.

What happened was that after Lyubka went off to the second camp and left me alone, Levan was sitting by the camp-fire. He wasn't like the other boys. He was married too, with a silver wedding-ring on his finger in the shape of two snakes divided by a deep split. The split was in the middle, with two identical snakes on each side. At first I thought it was two rings, like friendship rings, then I saw it was just one, split down the middle.

"Kissing's fine, just don't neck!" Lyubka says to me. To me! That was rich, coming from her! There's no point arguing with her though, she'll only start shuddering and calling you names. It's pointless. If she sees a black-marketeer with something she likes, she has to buy it, she'll go down on her knees for it. Then she'll say, "You were right, he cheated us." But it's pointless to argue with her, she'll only shout and shudder, it's best to let her have her own way. So after she shudders and shouts at me about not necking with Levan, I finally manage to calm her down and we go to the club – the farm-workers have a club there – and we're sitting on a bench, the lights are low, our lot are out in front, and Lyubka and I are sitting on the last bench, and she says: "Listen, Lariska, why do we have such a hard time? Look at us, we're the prettiest here – the tallest, the prettiest, the best dressed!" And she lunges at me and gives me a kiss. An obscenely long kiss, the moron. They're all looking at us, and Lyubka's gazing at me like she's drunk and can't tear herself away from me. Lyubka's pretty, but our boys thinks she's funny. Not funny ha-ha, just sad. They treat me the same way too, but I don't give a toss somehow. They just don't interest me now, because of Lyubka.

Levan was telling me all about his little girl. He has this daughter, and she's the only thing he loves. He says, "When you and me are married, I'll get three hundred roubles a month and teach her languages and you'll probably laugh at me."

I have trouble imagining this life – me, Levan, his

daughter, languages. What about my daughters? But I don't ask, I'm too distracted by Lyubka and her night adventures in the fields. Apparently she ditches our drunk girls and gets herself there all on her own. God, she's irresponsible. Think of all the farm hands and the wolves out there, circling around and sniffing at our Lyubka. We leave for Moscow in the nick of time.

Back in Moscow, I have this dream. I dream I'm going into a room which I know, because I've been there before. It's crowded, with lots of fat old women in there. I sit on a chair, and I know I have happiness, and these women are there because of my happiness. Then Levan comes in. He's just behind me and I don't see him, but I know he's there because everyone falls silent. And my happiness comes from him. I turn to face him, and I see him standing there – no, he's sitting too, and I get up and go to him and say: "See, Levan, it's happened exactly the way I wanted it."

But he says nothing, just slumps back as though he's dead, his head tipped back, his eyes closed, his lips half-open with pain, unable to speak. I start shouting and pulling him, not caring if it makes him angry, but his body just follows my movements, except that his face is all contorted with tears. This is my first dream about Levan.

Next day he comes to see me, and we have a lovely time sitting together dreaming of how we'll live, and we kiss, and he tells me he loves me. That evening Lyubka rushes over and we go to a bar, but we don't stay long and come back to my place to discuss our lovers. Then that night I have another dream. Lots of people again, all shouting at the tops of their voices. I break away from them and argue with them, and again Levan is sitting there, half-dead, on a sort of bench. I push my way over to him, and a woman attacks me in the doorway, and blood spurts from my leg and my ribs.

"What are you sitting there for, Levan?" I shriek at

him. "It's blood! My blood!"

He says nothing, and again it's as though he's been taken over by an alien force, and he gives himself up to its movements, and his face is contorted with tears. I finally manage to get to him and show him the blood gushing from my leg, and when I tell him to look, he looks. But if I hadn't told him to, he'd have sat there nodding and shaking his head and screwing up his face. He looks at my leg but he doesn't *do* anything. Then I take his hand and put it on the wound, and say, "Stop the blood." And because I'm holding his hand there, it stays. But little jets of black trickle through his weak-willed fingers, running down his arm to his elbow, which really freaks me.

That evening I say to Lyubka: "You and me are going to die, for sure."

Lyubka loves this, and she throws herself at me saying: "Darling Larisochka, that's so great! Let me kiss you! I love you so much, no one else loves you as much as I do! I think you're beautiful. Levan's an idiot. He's married. And ugly! Ugh! A peasant. You and me will lie in the same coffin together, all young and beautiful, like little twins!"

"So what about Sasha?" I say.

"I'll ring him tomorrow," she says. "I can wait. But now you and me are going to die."

Then I dream about Levan one more time. Again there's all these angry people talking about him and asking how it happened, and I push through the crowd and see him standing there in some doors, facing slightly our way but more into the middle of the room where he's just come from, and it's all dark and they're holding him, just showing him to us, and he's swaying on his weak legs and he can't help smiling at all our light and noise. I know I must call him, and from the dark room they order him to answer, quietly, faintly, lifting his head and whispering something. And I love him very, very much, more than I've ever loved anyone in my life, with a love I will never in my life understand, and all I can think of is how to remember this love and do something with it. And I'm thinking this really hard, and I take my eyes off Levan in the doorway, swaying timidly and against his will out of the darkness towards us. And I think, "What's it all for? Is this the way to live? Find a good bloke, have kids, yes – but this?" And when I look up again there's just an empty doorway, open a crack, with no Levan, just a wisp of smoke at the bottom.

I wake up and go to college. I can't look at Levan. By now we're not talking. He's avoiding me, spending all his time with his wife. He's scared of me too. So Lyubka and I go for a walk. It's really warm and she has on the same jacket she wore at Black Earth. We're walking down the street, and all the guys are eyeing us, and Lyubka's getting drunk on their looks and strutting along like a tart with her hands in her pockets, and suddenly she pulls out this ring. Then we remember Black Earth. Lyubka starts trembling. "Remember Black Earth, Larisa," she says, "God, I'll die of love."

We look around and see a second-hand shop. "Let's go in," she says cheekily. "Maybe we'll get a couple of roubles for coffee. We can sit down."

There's no point arguing, so in we go. Lyubka hands over the ring, and the old bloke at the window picks it up and peers at it. He peers and peers. I get fed up, and say, "Where are we going to sit down here? Let's go to a bar."

Then the old bloke looks at Lyubka and says, "Come over here, my girl."

So she goes up to him, and he says something to her. She shrugs, and we leave. He told her to come back tomorrow, apparently.

But she can't make it, so they come for her instead in a car with a guard, and they take her back to the shop. They blather on. Lyubka goes mad, lying through her teeth about everything to do with the ring. In the end they take the ring off her anyway and instead of giving her money – well, it's a pretty weird story. Lyubka and her whole family are all living off the state now because of that ring, and they've been told that all her children and grandchildren will live off the state too.

We have all we want now. Lyubka is fat because she eats more than anyone I've ever seen – she eats whatever you give her. We don't know what to do with ourselves, because she refuses to study all day "at some lousy college", as she puts it, which means she spends all her time now with Sasha. And Sasha behaves really oddly. When he heard about the ring and living off the state he said: "I never want to see you again, you bitch."

Then Levan comes over.

I didn't know he'd come, I wasn't expecting him. He just arrives at the door, takes off his coat and walks into the room. It feels strange to see him. He just walks into my room, goes to the table, sees a book, puts out his hand – and suddenly there's something sparkling on his finger, all rough and strong. I jump back thinking, "He can't be wearing a ring, especially a signet ring. I know he's Levan, but he has taste. What's going on here?"

I didn't understand that moment. Something rough and powerful flashed before my eyes, then I looked closer and I saw it was his silver wedding-ring. It had flashed just the same way before but now it looked somehow different, as though the silver had spoken to me and now was growing cold and dull on his finger. The two snakes were Levan and the wife he didn't love, and the split between them was me, whom nobody loved. And I understood everything. Everything. I understood that because the ring was made like that and Levan was wearing it, nothing would happen. Nothing. I don't know how to explain it, but nothing will happen. Nothing. Never.

Cold

As for how I came across the imbeciles – well, I had to make money for jeans. I told Mum: "You and your boyfriends spend everything on booze while I go around with nothing on. I'm getting a job."

"Fine," Mum said. "I'm not stopping you."

So I found a job as a cleaner at the theatre. The only problem was when we had to tip the water out. Our forewoman told us: "Try to throw it near the gutter, girls, or we'll have an icy patch spreading over the pavement and people will fall."

But who wants to run out to the gutter? Specially in the freezing cold, all hot from the theatre, with nothing on under your overalls. So of course we all chuck the water right by the doors – open the door, fling out your arms with the bucket and hurl it out. Then one day I notice this imbecile hanging around the theatre. His name is Uncle Leva. That shocks me a bit. I have a boyfriend called Leva, and now here's this imbecile called Leva. The thing is, he's tall too, almost the same height. It's revolting. It makes me sick when some really inferior type gets called Leva or Andrei – it's like a good name wasted. Why can't they call them Vasya or Kolya or something?

So right from the start I feel this sort of antipathy, which I can't hide because I don't know how it got there.

They keep handing this imbecile bottles, and I realise they're feeding him, and the reason they have him there is because the theatre used to be an old church. The belfry and another little church building are still there, and they've gradually become part of the theatre.

So, what a moment! They're putting on *The Robbers*, and they've brought out the cross to dry. They lean it against the wall of the little church building – a fine cross as big as a man. The gutter is right opposite, so I run past the cross three times with my slops. And suddenly, what's this, God's face is moving! I don't know if it's just the way the light is falling, because the dusk comes on quicker in winter, or if something horrible is going on! There's a puddle right near the cross, and I can't get close to it because I only have a pair of slippers on my bare feet. But I go to the edge of the puddle to see if everything is all right. The cross is standing there with its papier-maché God all covered in black paint. His stomach has ripped open, so the stage-hands have nailed a piece of wood there and painted it again, leaving it to dry, but you can still see the cotton-wool poking through the cracks where the muscles are, and a couple of nails have been hammered into the hands so they won't fall off. What I don't understand is why they don't paint those nails, sticking out all shiny and new. And what about the nails in his stomach? Couldn't they make a new God? Surely he'll slip off his cross at the climax of the performance, and the audience won't half stare.

So I'm standing by the puddle and suddenly I notice the imbecile standing there all covered in snow like a statue, watching me from a distance. How does he live, I wonder. What does he do at home? When does he eat? What does he feel? He's standing there rocking and swaying as though someone has pushed him and he's about to fall, but he doesn't, he just wanders off.

I've run out with the slops and the ground is all slippery and the snow is falling. What with the hot steam from our water below and the snow falling above, it's like hell – and God drying against the wall. And accidentally I look at him again, and I see his face move! He keeps moving! It drives me mad! He seems to move forward out of the dusk, through the whirl of snow, straight towards me. I'm not mad. It's not a real face of course, just smears of black, with bulges for the nose and mouth, all sticking out so you can see it from the stage – what it looks like close-up doesn't matter. And suddenly it's not just any old face, it's a special face! Perhaps the falling snow has made the air come alive – move, cast shadows or something, I don't know. Then I think either he's really looking at me and this is some kind of miracle, or I'm completely sane, not mad at all, and it's just a simple misunderstanding. So to hell with it, I walk in my slippers through the puddle. The puddle's all hot from the slops we've chucked there from the theatre, and I splash over it and across the snow, my feet freezing, right up close to the cross. And then I realise it's the snow. I thought it must be something like that – something from nature making him move as though he had a face. But what happened was that the snow filled in all the cracks, and that's what makes him look so scary, moving around with his eyes shut, covered in snow, and all those wrinkles... As though he was, well, dying. The bastards. I reach out to brush the snow off him, and my rubber glove is slippery and there's this revolting noise that makes me gag. I can't stand that noise. So I take off my glove and rub my hand over his eyes, his cheeks, his mouth and beard. Then I step back – and who should be standing there but our imbecile?

He's so t-a-ll, old Uncle Leva. He has a big nose, eyes popping out of his head like boiled eggs, and wrinkles that sag just like God's. He's so disgusting I'd only touch him with my bare hands if he was buried in snow. He wears this haughty, spiteful expression all the time, and he goes around looking frozen. The only time he looks happy is when he's sitting with the workers in their room, because it's warm in there, with the telly, people, hot tea. When he just hangs around he looks like nothing on earth. As though he's the most important person here, when he's an imbecile who can't speak, who people give bottles to. He's congenitally inferior – I'd like to know if he dreams, and if so, what about. I tried to talk to him once, but he didn't react. People are all the same to him, just a mass of different movements. Call his name and he'll call back, though. He'll swing around, moo like he's dying and lumber after his name. I saw him do it once. He mooed like something inside him was falling apart and all the bits were being ground up. Then I saw him staring at me angrily, as though I were stealing his bottles. I spat to show him what I thought of him, and left. Am I just imagining it, or does this imbecile really hate me? How can he, he doesn't know anything, he can't tell people apart, and why me? He must be living here on charity – maybe he'll make something of himself yet?

So I finish the cleaning and throw out the last bucket, and Uncle Leva's standing there like a machine. Why doesn't he sit indoors with the workers? Out here it's snowing a real blizzard, our water's steaming, and he's squelching around in the slush like a lost soul. I open the door, fling out my arms and hurl the water. I don't run to the gutter of course, like our forewoman tells us, I just do as the other girls do. And all of a sudden the imbecile lets out this roar, picks up a stone and chucks it at my head! I duck. The stone whizzes over me, straight into the glass doors. Smash! The imbecile roars even louder, twisting his lips and goggling at me. I go mad. That stone just missed my head, behind me there's glass everywhere, and two feet in front of me is this crazy idiot.

"Holy Mother!" I say, grabbing my bucket and running. I say nothing to our forewoman. Nor does the imbecile, of course. I never tell anyone why I work here only a month, take my seventy roubles and scram.

Next day I wear a hat in case he tries to smash my

head in again, and as I'm taking out the water I hear our forewoman giving someone a ticking off. I tip back my hat to listen. A slow, thick voice answers her, like something out of the abyss, but with that wheedling tone you use for the boss. I can even make out the words.

"I promise it won't happen a second time, Flora Mikhailovna," it says, like some subterranean element begging our Flora Mikhailovna's forgiveness.

Blah, blah, blah, Flora goes, but I get her drift – the workers have a drink, the cleaners get drunk, etc, etc.

I get the water really hot, pour in the soap-powder and stir it up into a nice thick foam so Flora won't moan at us for not using powder. Then I carry it out, taking care not to slop hot water on my feet and hoping to slip past Flora while she's yelling at someone else, so she won't make me do the stairs. But then our figure-skater swoops out in person, looking really furious and followed by the skiver, who's droning on and still answering back. Flora sees me and waves at me to stop, which means I'll have to do the stairs after all. Then she goes on: "You see you keep promising, and it's all for nothing!"

Then out shuffles the imbecile with his angry, sagging face, as if his wrinkles were pulling it downwards. I wonder who she's shouting at behind him, and suddenly Flora looks at the imbecile and says: "This is the last time I'm telling you, Leva!"

And Leva opens his mouth and howls: "The last time, Flora Mikhailovna! That's right!" And he shifts around free and easy, and says: "How can you shout at me, Flora Mikhailovna, I'm your little darling!"

And Flora says: "That's enough now Leva, take the keys and start work."

And the imbecile takes a bunch of keys in his limp, floppy, imbecile hand – not one key, a whole bunch of them – and he sticks out his lips all offended and says: "Don't you shout at your little Leva any more."

"All right Leva, now get back to work," says Flora and

turns to me. "And you can clean the stairs."

But I... I drop the bucket and run back up the stairs, fall on a step and start yelling, scared and horrified. He works here! He has work papers, and he speaks!

Back home I lock myself in my room and for some reason I couldn't stop crying. I didn't even notice where the night went, I was just sitting there and it suddenly grew light, so light. I looked out of the window and the sky was blue as blue, blue like a miracle, blue like spring, blue like it never is in winter. I stood by the window and it hurt my eyes to look at it. I was just going out when a wave of warm air blew over me and knocked me sideways. Then another wave, warmer, then a sea of warmth gushing in, and it grew still brighter. The whole room was flooded now with sun and light, and it was very hot.

My mum was in her room getting ready to meet someone. Her footsteps sounded light and happy, like I'd never heard footsteps sound before. And as she clicked her heels around her room, I sat in mine with more and more light pouring in, as though they were testing how much it could take, and at first it was lovely and warm, but then it grew hotter and it started to burn.

The heat went into all the corners of my room and grew white-hot, and behind the wall, light as a breeze, sounded the footsteps of my mother, so innocent, so close.

If I move I'll get scorched, because the heat is pouring over me. If I even change position it will burn me. I'm just thinking this when there's a little tinkling sound of splintering glass and the real heat floods into my room. At this moment I jump up, yell and throw myself towards Mum: "Mum, what's happening! I could have been burnt up!"

Mum says, "Take an aspirin and stop being stupid!" And she goes off, so delicate looking, clicking on her way to meet her bloke.

Flowering

It was early in the year, cold and slushy underfoot, and
spring was around the corner. A beam of sunlight fell
from the sky, piercing me as I stood beneath it. I stumbled
back into the modest dampness, but the joy of the beam
had entered the sap of my soul and flourished there. Small
but vigorous, it lay across my soul, bifurcating and turning
my blood to gold. Love flowed, death had no existence,
cruelty was shunned, breathing and walking happened of
themselves. Yes, we truly exist!

On the frozen corner of the boulevard, frozen twigs
were being sold. People bought them and carried them off
down the street. Beneath the red skin of the larger twigs
slept a kindergarten of tiny pink flowers. I took one and
checked to see if it had flowers. "I'll take five," I said. As
I grasped hold of the twigs, hard and cold in their red
skin, I knew the world was made for life. Just stand them
in a jar of plain tap-water, and they will slake their thirst
and froth with pink flowers. This doesn't happen by
accident, it's been dreamed up for people to show them
the beauty of the world, which includes in its embrace the
lowliest reptile.

Gulping mouthfuls of wind, I tore back to my eternally
sad home, scored with veins of black blood. Stepping
gingerly in the darkness and brushing against spiders with

my feet, I gently drowned in dust as I felt my way along the corridor. Lodgers groaned in the walls. Suddenly old Khazina pounced out at me, lunging at my chest, covering me with curses and hatred. I jabbed the twigs at her to ward her off, and she defended her eyes. Knotted like a piece of old rope, the old woman had eyes like zircons.

"I'm not poking your eyes, just the opposite!" I yelled.

"I hate you! I don't believe you!" growled the tiny woman with big feet.

"Stop blazing at me, and listen – these are for you, two whole twigs!"

"What for?"

"I'll show you. Have you a jar in your room?"

"I've a vase."

Look at you – your room's like death, your bed's for crawling into, not nestling. A blanket, a table, a chair – I don't understand, you work hard all your life, your family lives in pink buildings with antiques, aquariums, tapestries, drapes, orchid-patterned wallpaper, rugs with tropical butterflies, and they've long forgotten where it all came from and who it belonged to, now that it's theirs. They have silky dogs and children stuffed with vitamins, they adore the ballet, they have shelves full of books, they've forgotten their roots, they have Sèvres ornaments, family heirlooms – why have you got nothing? You didn't write from the heart, about the small, poor people, you threw yourself into the honest life of the millions. But I mustn't complain, I'm not in prison, I'm not dead, I've been allowed to live with millions of my grey-faced comrades next to the pink buildings, sitting on their grass and dreaming at their windows till they drive us away. But now look what you can do. You can put these twigs in water, go to sleep and close your zircons with their thin lids. Sleep one night, two nights, till the twigs have drunk all the water from the vase, then lift your eyes and your terrible face will behold not a sewer or a boiling kettle or a razor-blade, but a garden full of flowers.

"It'll never work!"

"Just wait and see. In this tiny chewed-up room the spring will show you a little V-sign of flowers, and a ray of sunshine will fall through your window, creeping from the sky to your bony feet and into the flowers. I shall put my flowers in water too, I too shall wake up in my God-forsaken room, pressed on all sides by hungry lives, and I too shall have a garden. Good night!"

That night Khazina appeared to me in a dream and questioned me, as though in competition with me, about the growth of the twigs and how long they would take to flower. During the day we would bore our flatmates stiff talking about the swelling of the twigs, how much air to give them, the kindness of the sun and whether or not to wash the floor. Khazina said not to smoke in my room – or they would die.

One morning I awoke and kissed their little mouths. Trembling, I knocked on Khazina's door. She opened it and understood everything, and we hurried to my room.

"How are they?" she blurted out as we went.

"Pink as manicures."

She stared at them for a long time. There were three twigs, placed far apart, two of them already in bud. She looked and looked, then she went out, her eyes on the floor, zircons gleaming behind their thin lids.

"Be patient, yours will flower soon," I said, and she nodded into the distance.

At that moment something happened to her. She closed in on herself, lost her anger and overwhelmed all of us with her sadness.

I spoke simple words of reassurance to her. "If they were snakes, I'd charm them with a pipe," I said, touching her smooth twigs, and something in her gurgled, because she was ninety years old but she was still a girl.

"Otherwise it makes no sense," I liked repeating to her, and I cut open my breast so the warmth of humanity would flow and help them to blossom.

Over the years Khazina's sadness passed and she became spiteful again, snarling and spitting in the saucepans, splashing disinfectant about, wheezing in my face and writing to the police about me. Once she vowed never to forget people. The zircons gleamed.

I hugged my happiness to myself. All around me was howling and stinking, but I hugged my happiness like a candle in the wind. Then one night in a dream a simple truth was revealed to me, and I knew that after Khazina's death she would not be buried, but that they would prize open her coffin in the morgue to discover the curve of her spine. Bits of her would be chopped off and sent to a medical school, other bits would lie in the fridge waiting for the next generation of doctors, and still others would be pickled in jars and sent off round the country as teaching aids for medical students.

I wiped away the tears from my dream. I wanted to tell her to make sure she was buried, but I didn't know how. I lay in the early dawn twilight pleading not to be frightened by any more terrible truths. But to my pleading they hurled the last bloody truth, which makes you scream and roll on the floor.

I pulled the blanket off her. She didn't remonstrate with me, she just waited sullenly, the zircons gleaming like new and lighting up her face. Hurling off the blanket, I rushed to the window, snapped the twigs into pieces, grabbed the vase by its throat and tipped it over the radiator. The groan was heard all over the building. Then I raced up to her again and hauled her from the bed. I saw the dent in the mattress where she had been lying. My brain flooded with heat as I pushed her against the wall. Flashes exploded in my head, the plaster screamed from the friction and there was a smell of shit as my voice hurtled against the wall: "You stupid cow, you'll never get your fucking flowers now!"

Unrequited Love

Like a hulking cloud. Like rush-hour. Like insulting the
army. Like getting up at six in the morning. Like losing
your purse with five hundred dollars, compromising
letters, all your papers and your visa. Like a rumour in a
communal flat that someone else is to be moved in. Like
seeing half a pigeon on the pavement, a dog being beaten,
a child being beaten. Like a missing person announcement.
Like a story from a children's home. Like night anxiety.
Like envying those you love most. Like them envying you,
their eyes judging you as they speak, their words twisted
like after a road accident. Like spitting in a beggar's cap,
like despising national minorities, like being afraid of
them. Like loving nobody in the world. Like sitting in
prison, waiting for the summer. Like silence on the
telephone, and you're afraid it's *them*, but it's not them –
it's you, Aleksei Orlov, but I call you Oleksei.

Oleksei, you drift up from the night shift of your
factory, out of the limitless expanse of the factory dawn.
The black chimneys belch smoke, the red ovens roar,
hellish constructions clank, there's nowhere for a stray cat
to hide, even in the dusty calico of the Red Corner, now
forever closed. No bench to sit on, no chair. You descend
into your factory each night and put on your work-clothes
so no speck of dust from this life will touch the factory's

sadness. You're alive – but it's only half a life, and I can't even call you by your real name, so hateful are you to me.

Large and wooden, with a dull face and spectacles, you seem blind, deaf and dumb, untouchable and unsmellable, without hands, legs, torso, teeth or hair, without address or voice. Without your idiot heart.

While everyone is sleeping, you work. While everyone is working, you wander the world in search of me. And I am always sleeping. I sleep when you work, and I sleep when everyone else works. I don't exist. I haven't been born, I only know I must sleep.

Why did you give me that little red bag with the gold design? I know what that design meant.

Oleksei Orlov, you keep coming to see me, but I have a family. You overshadow us with your sadness. You turn up while we're relaxing and chatting in the sun, and we become silent and withdrawn, fawning on you, making sure you're comfortable, giving you our favourite things to make you feel at home. Our little girl hands you her best toys, my husband provides political discussion and good tobacco, I offer female requests for intelligent advice. But it's impossible to make you happy. You bring rolls for us to eat with our tea. I don't want tea with you. I don't want anything with you. When you're with us, my own husband dares not sit next to me for fear of hurting your feelings.

It's all my fault. You were floundering, and I happened to treat you kindly that summer. I didn't know you would destroy yourself for me. What have you dreamed for in your life? What crazy visions? What cavorting worlds in your soul? What clouds in your head? Tell me, you give us so little to go on! You have a nice family, a clever wife, a pale little boy named Misha. Once I timidly praised your son, and you told me he hated me. Your glasses flashed when I grew upset. So his childish heart understands, is that it? And when I was playing with him and said to you: "We've been playing, Olyosha – we have a secret!"

your face darkened. Why was that? You love your good family, but you ache for me, and I am rubbish, so your innocent child must hate me? You said: "Yesterday I saw someone run over. I thought it was you lying dead on the pavement." Surely it was a man who was run over? How could a dead man remind you of me? Where is the resemblance!

When I complained to my husband, he stood up for you and said my coldness must be hard for you, and I should be more sensitive. But it's hard for me when you sit there, your heavy heart groaning in your aching breast, your glasses gleaming like instruments of torture as you smile crookedly at me.

"How nice to see you!" I say. You've just finished the night-shift, the factory is still roaring in your head, and you long for a more interesting life. Please believe me! I've been there, too, and I learned that there's nothing better in the world than to save up patiently for the summer, go off to the seaside or the country and say your humble thanks to the world. You'll understand what I mean if you manage to survive.

Now you emerge exhausted into the sunshine. That's what it's like as a shift-worker. So either find another job or accept this one. Go home in the morning to your sunny flat overlooking the trees, take a shower, eat the buckwheat porridge wrapped up in a towel to keep it warm, lie down in smooth sheets and drift slowly and sweetly into sleep. Your wife is at work, your son is at school, the cat pads around silently catching moths, and you sleep. I want less sadness in the world. Sleep slowly and sweetly, and dream of our country, rising from her knees and sweetly reaching out to the world with all its children and its old people, its young and its middle-aged. And there is no more sadness. And we two are strangers.

Unrequited Love

Closer to Rest

It was like this after the war, Marina, remember? Half the house left standing, they couldn't be bothered to rebuild it, just a lick of paint and a patch-up. A short life and a merry one. Sometimes I feel like hanging myself.

Leningrad's full of invalid homes, like that one on Old Nevsky...

Look Marina, there's a café! Come on, let's have a coffee – if there is any. Yes, there's coffee! Salads, brandy, coffee, a slice of bread – bread I said, not blood! Stop shouting, stupid! We'd better get out of here, you're crazy, like the rest of this town. You're always yelling – you never stop! Now drag your leg, tip your hat over your ear, that's right, yell and walk. Where are we going, Marina?

You said you wanted to see the graveyard. If you don't want to, I'll go anyway since I'm here. There it is, at the end of that street, see, by the palace. Drag your leg now, talk, yell.

What's in the graveyard then, bodies? Look, the church is closed, and the graveyard too. Whose are those graves in front of the church?

Don't go, Lena, they'll suck your blood – they're soldiers' graves, not saints'. You know what, they picked the plaster off Saint Kseniya and tested it, and it turned out to be full of energy! They proved it – they had instruments. It's cold here. That flowering lilac is a graveyard lilac. The graves are old, everything's been sucked out of them by underground waters, light clean bones under the stones.

The lilac's not a graveyard lilac, it's a plain old Petersburg lilac – your lilac, Marina. It's May, but it's so cold I could weep. I'm going, let's have another drink, let's not go to Kseniya. You said you'd take me there but I kept talking, you've lost your memory, you forgot I wanted to see Kseniya. Look at you – second-class invalid, dragging your foot, from a distance you look okay, close-up you looked okay twenty years ago. My hands are frozen in this silk coat with no gloves. It's a good coat, but wrong for this weather, it cost a lot but I'm not dressed right. I'm all on my own now, Marina, everyone in my family's dead and gone. What shall I ask Kseniya? Bones, will you visit me? I used to visit people, but I'd leave in tears and they wouldn't ask me back. Young people sculpt dinosaurs, they drink wine and enjoy themselves, clever, curly hair, bright colours – I can't stand it. We just get cold. I'll wrap myself up in my coat. I don't know, the games young people play now – and the dancing. We're too old for all that.

Fine, let's shuffle back to your place and play grannies. Look at those darkies, all black in the cold. Why the hell did they leave their hot countries in the first place? It's nice and warm in your room, fur rug on the bed, you stitched it together from old hats, patiently bending your head and humming, needle flashing. Let's snuggle under the rug together with a bottle of wine and warm up in clean sheets, all ripped and tattered. What are you doing on that chair-bed behind the cupboard? The glasses ping. The sky's sunny outside, but I'm stiff with cold. The sun's bright, the sun's high. I want an empty heart with a clear light backbone of memories, but I just can't stop squeezing the pus from it. What do you do with a heart like that? Chew the rug, steal your pension, spit in your face and

Closer to Rest

watch you tremble, invalid.

You say I'm the poorest person in Leningrad, but people are forever popping in for a rouble and a chat. Marvellous people they are, but washed up, drug addicts, they're all dying, nobody wants to know. I wrote to the government about our young people, Marina. No answer.

Last time I stayed with you there was a brothel next door. Natasha had men over, shouting all night like animals. I said fetch the police, and you wouldn't. "I can't sleep," you said, "but I won't call the police!" It made me feel ashamed of myself. Remember that family of beggars we saw in the underground? There was a little girl in a faded dress, ugly little thing, I didn't like her. She stared at me like children do – it annoyed me, only pretty children can stare at you like that. Remember Nastasya Filippovna's house in Dostoyevsky's *The Idiot*? I don't need to see it, I've lived there all my life. You've a good son, it's frightening how quickly he grew up – married, going bald already. We're washed up now, Marina. Come on, let's drink, forget our gloomy rooms, our made-up beauty and bad health, forget this sadness, the sadness of lonely old women eating the meat from the neighbours' saucepans, the iron bed which the police didn't discover, poor Nastasya Filippovna, alone and hungry for ninety years, fishing bits out of our saucepans, the witch. Look in the acid-bath, the iron bed unmade for three years, the police find the bed and make it with their young hands... Oh the sadness, poor Natasha, a new one every night but they're all the same, I don't call the police, she's from the Ukraine, Granny stayed in the village and gave birth to a pig, Granny's pig had a pig, it escaped to the forest, they just let them go there, it happens all the time, they don't feed them so they go wild – a wild, eight-legged creature running about the forest. People don't go to the forest now, they just stay at home waiting to die, they tidy up, wash the floor and sit there in clean shirts telling each other the creature will soon break out again, the tomb can't stop it, it hasn't the strength to hold back death, we bring it offerings and ask for more time, it's on our side, it does its best for us. The forest is alive with a strange two-headed beast, don't take the sad forest path, little cow, I don't want my grandmother to die churning butter, I'll take the sad forest path and look for strange flowers, the lilac which isn't lilac – why are there so many new flowers out this spring? It's never been like this before, I don't understand it, crooked branches alive with young sap, down, down the crooked path of spring, the forest doesn't realise it's different, or does it? Where is our little piggy eight-legs? It's weeping by the brook, go home now, little cow, go to Leningrad and good luck to you, take my pension, I don't need it, I've wonderful vegetables and many-legged animals, the cow's milk is pink as the sky, I'm telling you love, I saw it in the forest! Why have you come back so small? When you left you were a big girl, now you're my granddaughter, don't be scared, it's a new life, it only poisons the weak, I read about a baby girl once, born normal, developed okay, smiled before she was one, then her neck swelled up, they x-rayed it with special instruments, and it turns out she had another brain growing in her neck! Two brains in one child, playing and whispering in the dark together – she'll never ever be alone! It's a new life, everything growing huge, massive, legs, heads, eyes, it's a new life, don't be scared, it doesn't hurt us, it sustains us, I wasn't scared when I saw all the new flowers in the forest, I went to see if it's a flower curving and frothing so sweetly, and my temples hurt as I touched it but I wasn't scared, I didn't pick it – here, take some cash for your journey; the sadness, Marina, the sadness. Then I saw the branch of lilacs gleaming behind the gravestones, shying away from the beauty in dark, low-born horror. That's what the past is, spilling out all over the place, and our tour guides can hardly make out a word of it. What comes after us? Nothing. All gone. Dead, forgotten. That's why the lilac in the rain angrily shied away, the froth from a life that's gone, in the past, all our loved ones under the ground, young Pioneers milling around eating ice-creams in the cold, graves, walls, monks lived here once – children, look there's General Suvorov's grave. Why did you bring me here, the cartoons will be on soon. I'm cold, the flowers are wet, it's going to rain again.

What's this life of ours? It's all new, that's what. So I meet this passionate man, reckless and quivering, dressed in rags, young skin, rippling muscles, a janitor – a poet. So what, Marina? I can see the rags, the clumsiness, his wine, my wine. Because he's brushed with life, like that cold bush there bringing down the rain. He wants to live, he clicks his heels and the blood leaps to his heart. Living means a house, furniture, clothes, books, the orange light in our windows, but how are we supposed to live? He's passionate, I'm passionate, what's money? My mum's overweight, she has high blood-pressure but she lives on starch and fat, she saves all her money for me, I'm embarrassed to go out with her, everyone can see my expensive coat was paid for out of her pension, and her clothes all come from skips and friends. He has a wife too, loved her terribly. It's all in the past. But then if it's in the past, why does he call out for her at night? When he met me I shut him up.

Tell me, Lena, didn't you say this Ivan of yours was an Asian?

Yes, he's a Tartar.

Makes no difference – that's Asia. The last few years they've all been leaving Asia and moving into our basements. They surround themselves all their lives with icons, candles, eastern wisdom, all that stuff – they come on like prophets. I went to see one of them once, he never stopped talking, and if anyone interrupted he shouted at them. I asked him some questions and he quietened down and answered politely. Life's tough for them in Central Asia, that's why they all head for Russia. A couple of my girlfriends lived with two of them and got pregnant – one hanged himself and the other landed up in the bin. These are sick Asians. First the Asians will swallow us up, then the Negroes. That's what the astrologers say.

Oh Marina, that's the other Asia.

I don't know, Lena, perhaps I'm wrong, but they have a huge will to live. After I was ill I forgot everything – poems, songs.

I'm telling you, Marina, my Ivan's a harmless Asian, he's just neurasthenic. He has warm yellow skin and he helps his wife, he gives her good money. He loves life. He's still partly living for her, see. For who? For life. Engaged or married, that's how they are, they're in love with life. They've a daughter too. He helps her. I didn't know where he was getting the money from, then I saw he was selling his books. His own, of course, he doesn't touch mine – he cares about his family, you see. He's tender and passionate. He has no special will for life, he just loves it.

That's how it is with them – life, they get drunk on it. My husband was terrible, madly jealous he was, I liked it at first but then it wore me down, Lena, it wore me down. He must be a Doctor of Sciences by now.

My Tartar's not a doctor, he has a scar under his armpit, he has a little daughter, a life-wife – no, honestly, that's what they say. I love you, life. He married for life, not thinking perhaps, out of convenience. At night he shouts out as though he's saying goodbye to life, during the day he's out drinking. He's full of love. "I'm looking for love, darling," he tells me. I'm terrified for him. If he's beaten up or put inside, life will have the privilege of crying and saying goodbye, not me. Come on, Marina, drink up, it's nice drinking with you, you're not drinking. He says, "You can't get away from life, darling." There he is on the ring-road outside Moscow, spring's bubbling up and he's looking around with red eyes – who are we, how do we live? I almost went schizo, Marina, like another me, two-faced, red-eyed, I had to go down the crooked paths of sadness into the forest, to the thing with eight legs.

Here, I'll just get that bottle of my son's. Here Lena, have a drink of this. Drink, it's hours before my train. It seems as though everyone needs something of your husband, Lena. It's not true, of course, but you know what I mean.

Squeeze the pus from my heart, Marina, I'm not drunk yet, I've lost Ivan the Tartar, I've forgotten the smell of his skin, lilacs and water, the body's secrets are closed to me – because he's married to life! We lived together all winter, we lay with each other through the early spring, we listened to the world coming to life on the edge of Moscow – orange windows, ground floor flat – we led his little girl down the crooked spring paths to my dark Tartar husband, my eyes red with tears but my heart light – the clean-washed spine of memory in my gentle heart, the pus running out to underground rivers of tears, and our daughter, the daughter of our life and your Tartar darkness, wandering along the spring paths. I knew the summer would throw us apart, Marina, I just knew. In summer, life rules with terrible omens of stifling pollen, pink evenings and dust. Who is this two-headed creature beside you, darling husband? Send it away to the forest of eight-legged things, find yourself a bare-footed girl, let her eat from your hand, let this thing hide in its lair, curving and foaming into the earth, I don't want to give it life. I am sweet and gentle, breathe for me, my darling husband, ringed like a bird. This is how it ended: "Dear Ivan, sensing the tremor which is the will to live and which made your red heart swell in the spring, I shall let you go to save you from the shame of wondering how to leave me. Go to Kazan and organise things, young people are spilling their blood, stop the blood, you're ringed by life like a bird, people listen to you, speak simple words to the dark Tartar people, make them stop, make them stop, make them give up cannibalism, take up agriculture and sing national songs. Goodbye, your L." Who's that shout-ing?

It's Natasha's blokes. We're drinking here, they're drinking there. It's terrible, they'll be at it all night. You said it was the white nights already, but look, it's getting dark. It's only May, the white nights aren't till June.

How many times can you start again – that's what I need, to start again. Each time something is wrong – it's something else. You walk down Nevsky Prospect wanting nothing for yourself – it's not so much wanting nothing as looking at everything and understanding what people want. There's a little girl of twelve in patterned tights and open sandals. Her toes are pink in the cold, like my fingers. She's not dressed for the weather, the Nevsky toes of her feet are freezing, the men see but she doesn't care, life smiles at her with its red eyes, and her Nevsky toes are pink. She's a bold girl, she gets to the traffic-lights first and takes us with her. When I arrived here yesterday at six in the morning, a young woman in stockings was asleep on the stairs in your hall. Drunk, of course. I was surprised the hard stairs didn't hurt her young ribs. As I stepped over her I thought, look at this young woman – but then I've lived too, Marina, we've both lived.

I go into the kitchen to rest my leg – I know I'm an idiot, I'm always lighting the wrong gas. I just have to rest my leg. When I was ill, Lena, my husband couldn't hide his happiness. You know, he was overjoyed that I'd had it, he wanted to crush me, trample me, he wanted me to die.

I'll tell you something, Marina, we're not strong enough, and life doesn't like weaklings. When you shouted on Nevsky today about pay toilets I nearly flipped my lid – I could just see us walking along, me dressed up to the nines in my nice coat with an idiot on my arm. Mentally you're excellent, Marina, you've got an excellent mental illness which melts the cruelty of our life into the land of milk and honey. It's good to be sick, to drive the pain

Closer to Rest

from your system, to let everyone get close to you, take nothing from life and not see dangerous people. Since you can't hurt anymore, you go out to everybody, however seedy they are, you talk to them, you ask questions, you give them cash for the journey – the beautiful woman in you has died, but there's lots of warmth left in you. Just now you said even the plaster was alive, so some things don't know death. Our Kseniya lived the life of a rich young girl. When her fiancé died she woke up, went out into the air, looked around and started living. She saw people's pain and she embraced it, she lived for everyone and she's still living to this day. A simple Russian story. So she became the poorest of the poor, and her life left her for others. Maybe it's like that with us, maybe we're the poorest of the poor, and the warmth has already left us and we don't know. It may even be that the Ukraine doesn't die. I feel so sorry for the Ukraine, Marina, it's such a rich land. Perhaps the other people won't die either, perhaps even the Tartars and the simple people of the Far North will flourish, like we dreamed, and nations will be woven into a wreath of oaks and corn-sheaves, and the Asians will swallow us up if that's what they want. We've no will left to live, anyway.

What do you want, Lena? Just ask me.

Leave me alone.

I shan't.

I'll be off then. I catch the train, what a laugh. A fat woman with red cheeks is sitting there beside a little chap: her son, I assume. I take a good look at him, he's tiny but not a dwarf, a typical town-planner, I'd say. It's cosy on the train, the sheets are nice and clean. I strip down to my underwear since the company's so pleasant – there's another chap with a lovely velvety voice, he gives us a funny look then goes into another carriage, and we have a good laugh! So I'm in my underwear, the company's pleasant, the train's slipping along, if only life was always like this – there's my bed, go to sleep, oh how sweet, I'm almost asleep, outside Moscow the train windows run past grass, pink eyes in the spring – hello husband, hello wife, life, where's our daughter? She's sleeping, the little daughter of life and dark Tartar blood. I know why you're so small, life laughs at you, people insult you, they don't respect you at work, you warily tread the warm path of life, looking around with shy delight, then milk flows into my heart and I prolong sleep. This hasn't happened for years, not since I was a child. A tiny man on a business trip, then a plump girl comes in and takes out her eyes, pink contact-lenses, scares me to death it does. Goodnight, everyone. The trees flash past my temples in the night, spring darts by without touching my hair, the earth trembles, I'm sleeping, flying over the earth, my hair streaming behind me and dragging by its ends a little man on a business trip with a briefcase. Next morning we take turns to wash and drink tea, we arrive on time, we shake hands and say goodbye. Back home I kiss everyone, ask Mama, "Did Ivan ring?" He hasn't. Mama says, "Lenochka, go and collect our food parcel, they said there'd be extra meat today." So off I go to the store.

Closer to Rest

Star-Boy

From the burning centre of Earth, heart of the magma, mother of our world, the heat of life rises into the sky. Without her we'd freeze. Our life, our towns and villages are all blueness and light – but if her blood cools we'll crash through the blackness of that terrible cosmic *kaput* – no life, no beginning, no end... I can't stop thinking about it.

I live in Russia – tough country, lots of snow in winter. When I was young I believed in Lenin – got married by the Eternal Flame, I did. I used to lie on the ground at night staring up at the sky – never saw infinity, though...

It was my son Yura got me into space. He was the first one up there – just tore through the blue membrane of life and into the emptiness. He saw there was no God there, just darkness, eternal darkness, the unseeing light of foreign suns. And when my darling boy came back, he said: "It's really true what our people say, Mama – there's no God!", and his blue eyes were laughing with pride.

I won't tell anyone why he disappeared and how they destroyed him, just that one day he couldn't take any more and he spat in Brezhnev's face for making him drunk. From that moment he vanished without trace, my only son, my Yura. Not even the fame of his snow-white smile could warm him. Covered in stardust he went hot and cold, and his brave eyes shone blue with laughter – Conqueror of the Universe! He went pale and started swearing and shouting at people and looking behind him. Even the sea was too small for him. The nights were the worst.

My darling boy spat in the old man's face for daring to say his people were happy. He knew it was wicked to tell people lies about happiness. He could see for himself there was nothing beyond the stars, nobody to tell: "We've built everlasting happiness for our people down there." Nothing but blackness, the emptiness of infinity, no one to see us, just a hellish hole, noiseless, airless, lightless, which could burst your heart like it burst the hearts of Belka and Strelka, those two dear little cosmonaut dogs. And when he spat at the great deceiver of the Russian people, the old man turned red and destroyed him without trace.

All we have is this lonely Earth, on which life just happened. Here we are, busy, earthy people alongside a lot of other warm soft creatures.

I've lived on my own since my son died, hidden myself away, no one knows who I am. Life's not easy or hard, frightening or happy. I greet every day with a thoughtful smile – I'm not greedy, like other earth creatures. My little pension covers my food and heating and keeps me in newspapers. But if they say things about space I rip them out, because it's all lies.

My flat-mate Orlov, our janitor, shouts at me for tearing up his mail. I say nothing. He lives his dull little life, scratching about on the surface of Earth and breeding goldfish in deep, green tanks. I don't stop him putting his tanks in our shared kitchen. I like to see the delicate water plants waving lazily in the water and the bright fishes darting around. I like their tiny gills. The fish aren't part of our life in the air, are they, yet the tiny things go round on same axis as us, never spilling a drop from their world.

Star-Boy

Oh, but sometimes my heart aches – it aches from Orlov's grim looks and his joyless working mornings. This cunning, lumpish man is young enough to be my son. When he was a defenceless baby lying swaddled up at the maternity home, a mystery, like every new-born baby, I was a strong young woman with big plans for my life. I knew we came into this world for brightness – otherwise why would we be born!

But it all turned out differently. Here's me, an old person with my scorched past, and there's Orlov, a stickler for the rules in this flat, an old young man already, pickled in sticky black wine – he's even going bald!

Whenever I go to our kitchen window and look up at the sky, he smirks, grabs the fish-pellets and bends over his shining midgets. He doesn't want to know about space.

I put my hand on my heart, go off to my room to sit on my bed and stare at the portrait of my son. I brush the dust off the red wax rose under his portrait with a special squirrel-fur brush which reaches its inner depths, and I fill a vase with water for it – the flower was never alive, but it deserves to be because of the unfading shine of its flaming petals. And my shining son looks at me through the glass of his portrait and says to me with a smile: "Thank you for the rose, Mama. Don't be afraid if your soul melts into tears of eternity again – shout it to the world, because I'm your son, and it was people and their inquisitiveness that cruelly sent me up there to be burnt up by the emptiness. They wanted to *know*, so they threw me up there! Tell everyone about it, shout the truth to them!"

At my son's words the glass sweats, then melts in the little spot of his breath, and when it disappears the portrait gleams with its cold, glassy shine, and the rose's blazing petals cry out about Eternal Glory!

Then I get up from my bed and go to the kitchen. Orlov peers at me and understands everything. "Lo-ord!" he says, and drops what's in his hand, though he doesn't notice. I take my hand from my heart and shout into those unbelieving eyes, full of anger and pain, I shout about the black infinity beyond the sky, where there is no life and nothing exists. Orlov yells back, waving his science fiction books at me and shouting out bits from them. But I laugh at him with a terrible laugh and tear the books up. He shouts about various things – he goes on in great detail about things that crawl, and things that fly and things with tentacles and hooks and bits like us, and they're all scattered around the planets of infinity – alive! I sadly contradict him. There's nothing up there, I say, not even with hooks on. There beyond the sky there's *nobody*.

True, I liked some of them, especially those porkie pigs – round like little loaves of bread, with happy blue eyes and pink ears. They're spoilt and they're sweet-tooths and they don't understand a thing – you have to repeat everything a hundred times! It makes me laugh when we talk about the sweetie people and their dear little lives, but I know Orlov's only telling me stories to make me laugh, so although it makes me sad, I deny them, mournfully, with a firm shake of the head. Then we start arguing again. We go on arguing until the dull Moscow morning turns dark. We argue about whether there's life around us or not, and then we stumble off to our rooms.

Next day Orlov hits the bottle, and then the long grey Moscow silence sets in, sticky with dark dusty-rusty wine and Orlov's nocturnal groans.

That's how we lived, year in, year out, until one day Orlov was visited by a small black woman from beyond the rolling line of the mountains. She instantly reminded me of something, and my heart missed a beat. But the memory passed and my heart grew calm again.

The mountain woman was holding by the hand her ten-year-old son. He was called Felix. Her name was Faina Dyrdybaeva. I wrote to the Housing Office and they told me there were no such people – they'd never heard of the Dyrdybaevs.

Then my noodles started disappearing from the saucepan. It reminded me of when I was young and I worked for the city council. I got big and bouncy, I saved up my salary and bought myself sweets, stockings, even "Red Moscow" perfume. When I had no money I was thin and flowing, like a delicate water plant which can survive without food, and lies pampered by the strong arms of the water.

I like to remember the sunlit days of my life on earth, when the sun over my head was still *whole*. I don't mind about the noodles, of course. Let the kid have 'em. They fish the noodles out of my saucepan and eat them, just like that, the white noodles dangling from their dark fingers as they put their hands to their faces to slurp them up. Then dark hairs started appearing in my hairbrush.

I know that every living creature secretly reaches out to each other. Thanks to the incomprehensible miracle of life. But nowhere, around our Earth ball, there's nothing. Thus, living thing must reach out to living thing.

I decided to talk to the woman, even though the Housing Office said she didn't exist. "Listen, Faina," I said, "your Felix – his hair's all down his back. He's a *boy*!"

She says: "Tomorrow we're going to the Mausoleum to see Lenin. Felix has been begging me to take him."

"You're not registered in Moscow, you've no job, your son's not at school, none of the kids in the yard will play with him because of his hair..."

"I *have* a job – at *Komsomolskaya Pravda*."

"And those hairs in my brush, are they yours or Felix's?"

"I've a child!" she says. "I'll go to the Moscow Soviet – our deputy'll get us a flat!"

I say: "Orlov will start drinking!"

"I'll get Orlov banged up!" she screams. "I've a child!"

Money or a few cups disappearing is one thing, but they pick my lock with a bit of wire. They twist it, the lock clicks, and they come right into my room. I get home at night, look up at my window and see the light of their torch hunting for things to steal. I stand in the dark yard and look up at my dark window; from one darkness I look into another, and in the upper darkness of my window runs a mortally frightened little beam of light. I know its sadness, its loneliness, its fear of dark, shadowy objects, as its hungry beam sweeps the emptiness for just one thing to call its own – even a stick of wood. But the shadows and the outlines are silent, frighteningly silent. I wait for the light to go out and the window to go blank, like in space, then I go in through the front door.

I had a little brooch with a leaf and a berry on it. The berry fell out years ago – pecked out by a sparrow, I think it was. I see Felix going out one day with the brooch gleaming on his new shirt, and I tell him the berry on it had been red, and a sparrow pecked it out.

"I'll have you certified!" screams Faina.

Felix looks at me with darting, bird-like eyes, and waits for the ambulance to come. But it doesn't. No red cross, no siren.

Because Faina has no residence permit, and Orlov won't betray me.

Orlov feels a bit funny about Felix and his strange clothes. But Faina loves Felix to shock people, she shrieks with laughter when they stare at him. Felix just shrugs and squeaks: "I want some sweets, Mum!"

She encourages him to embarrass people. Once Orlov went berserk when Felix came into the kitchen in his low-cut, crimson shirt, with his yellow collar-bones sticking out like they were crying.

Orlov looks daggers at me, and I say to him: "These people from beyond the rolling lines of the mountains have seen nothing but television all their life. And television shows nothing but operas and ballets. They like *Carmen* because the music's hot, and it's hot where they come from too. So *Carmen* is in tune with their desire for

Star-Boy

beauty – and it's beautiful Orlov, you must admit!"

"So now it's *Carmen*!" he says, getting up from the table, where the three of them are eating soup out of the saucepan. Faina guffaws: "Oh no, you're killing me! I'll die laughing! This is too much!" And so on. Looking at his mother, Felix joins in, yelping and squirming.

I go to my room and sit on my bed. Honestly, that red shirt of Felix's cut me to the quick. It did something to me, like when I first opened the door to that little tramp, his mother, and she raised her dark face to me and whispered: "I need a glass of water!" It reminded me of something, that red shirt – but what?

These new people in our life eat fruit with the peel on and make tea with hot water from the tap. Orlov's a Russian and a true Muscovite, he knows what's what, but he's too sozzled to care, he just bawls at Felix, "Son, son!" when everyone knows he isn't his son at all.

Felix peers up at Orlov, he knows he'll soon be on the road again with his mother, just like they were before. Felix seems to know more than his mother does, but he's in no hurry to speak. Of course they can stop wandering if Faina's deputy gives her a flat because of her child. Felix would have to have his hair cut then, because boys registered in Moscow can't wear their hair half-way down their backs.

But their darkness, it disturbs me, such deep, black darkness, it makes me shiver!

Once when I was young I travelled to the Caucasus. My heart nearly stopped when I saw those mountains looming over our meek Russian plains and reaching for the sky. I climbed one of them. I didn't know you needed special training and stuff, I just wanted to get to the top. When I couldn't get any higher I looked down and I gasped – I was standing on a rock – and that was it, nothing as far as the eye could see. The wind tried to blow me off, but I lay on the rock, curled up in a ball and waited to be rescued, quietly at first, then more noisily. At last some mountain people came. They bundled me into a reeking goatskin which was rough inside and scratched me, but it was better than the endless abyss, and in that skin they carried me down. They were black from head to foot, apart from their teeth. I was amazed. On the rock everything was white and blue. Stands to reason – the nearer you are to the sky, the brighter you are. Those mountain people shook me up. I couldn't understand why they were so black, surrounded by all that blueness.

I said to Faina: "You have a lot of light in the mountains. It's all blueness and white. You live practically under the sky!" I wanted to chat to her about her country – people always like that, and I wanted her to tell me about why they're so black, even though they live so near to the sky.

She said to me: "I work for *Komsomolskaya Pravda* – I'll write in and tell them you're scum!"

I looked at Orlov, but he'd grabbed the fish-pellets and was bending over his watery comrades.

"Hasn't Felix learned to read yet?" I asked.

"You heard what I said!" shrieked Faina. "The child's been pestering to take him to see Lenin!"

"Sod off!" Orlov shouted into his aquarium, then to me: "Sod off to your precious Yura and leave us to eat our supper in peace!"

Then Felix minced out like a Chinaman and stood in front of Orlov. He was shy – he liked looking at me, but he was shy.

I said: "I just want us to be friends!"

"Sod off, we don't want to be friends!" Orlov yelled.

When he starts yelling, it means he'll soon hit the bottle.

"Keep your hands off my wife and son!" he bawls. "You should have made friends before!"

Faina and Felix clung to his shoulders like little black moths, pressing their dark heads to his pale, frightened face.

Star-Boy

"Understand?" said Orlov.

I didn't reply. A vague notion suddenly flashed through my head, cutting me to the quick like Felix's crimson shirt, like my first glance of Faina; then it settled and melted at the bottom of my soul, leaving behind only irritation and muddle. "What's the matter with you? Cat got your tongue?" Orlov snapped. "What're you staring at?"

I raised my hand and signalled for them to be quiet. They fell silent. They went quiet, and I turned and went to my room to sit on the bed and bounce gently on the springs. But the thought didn't come back.

Yura was silent behind his glass. He slept, pale with exhaustion. I felt annoyed with him, but I didn't want to wake him, I just changed the water for his rose – I love it when fresh water sends silver bubbles to the sides of the vase.

That evening Orlov locked himself in the bathroom with a bottle of wine. He always feels like a chat after he's been boozing, so I knew he wouldn't be in there long. Sure enough, he soon came out of the bathroom all fresh and bright-eyed, his lips smeared with sticky black wine – it made the whole flat smell musty.

Faina had gone to the Moscow Soviet to see her deputy, but Felix was sitting in his room playing with his hair. He never played with toys, only his hair. I went out to the kitchen, because I always talk to Orlov. He started off by saying nothing. He gasped, his chest heaved, he cracked his knuckles and blew out his nostrils. Then he peered down into his fish-tank and said: "Hi, there!" At the sound of his voice the fish swam up. It looked as though he was kissing them, but they were just inhaling the fumes from his breath like he'd taught them. Then they swam off to their corners, trembling like Felix. Orlov tapped on the glass to get them to look at him again. I waited patiently. I knew we had lots to talk about.

Orlov raised his head from the tank and looked at me.

I met his gaze. He moved to a chair, sat down opposite me and poured out a glass of wine. I waited for the black wine to bring a red fire to his pale face. Swallowing the wine in three gulps, he put the sticky glass neatly on the table.

"So?" he said.

I said nothing. I'd no intention of changing my position.

Then, to my surprise, he talked about something else. "Listen, don't think I don't know what Faina's up to!" he said. There's nothing I could say to that. All I know is, they don't exist – the Housing Office told me.

"Faina's a vagrant," he says, "she's nowhere to live."

"If only we could live on other planets..."

"Sod off with your planets!" he yelled. "She needs to marry me to get her residence permit, understand?"

That was of no interest to me.

"And I'm going to, understand?" said Orlov.

"I understand!" I nodded patiently.

"No you don't, you don't understand a thing! Once she's got a room, I'll be out on the street!"

I didn't understand that. "Don't be ridiculous, Orlov, it's your house. Yours and mine, both together."

"Idiot! She'll get her permit and dump us – both together! She's artful – and I drink. I'll say nothing about you. She'll have us both put away, okay? She wants us out!"

Then I understood. "Better not marry her then, Orlov," I suggested.

"Well, I'm going to," he said, his face flushed with black wine.

And again it came to me, the idea I'd already tried to hold back but couldn't.

"Wait," I said, "Faina and Felix come from the rolling line of the mountains..."

"Can't you talk Russian?" Orlov flared up.

"But aren't I right?"

"They're bums, you mean? Yes, you're right there."

"I wish you wouldn't use those words, Orlov – bum, female dog..."

"You mean bitch?"

"Orlov!"

"All right, so they've come from beyond the rolling line of the mountains..."

"Which reach for the sky."

"Which reach for the sky."

"They can't though, Orlov!"

"Why not? What are you so happy about? More revelations?"

"Yes!" I cried out.

"What now? The mountains been whispering to you?"

"When I was young, Orlov, I got lost on the mountains..."

"I know you did! They dragged you half-dead off a rock. You were pregnant. That was clever! Pregnant and lost on the mountains. Jesus Christ!"

"I did it so my baby would be nearer the sky! And look what happened!"

"Please don't go on, that's enough!" Orlov whimpers.

"Don't interrupt me, then!"

"Okay, I won't!" he says eagerly.

"As you know, Orlov, the people who carried me down from the top of the mountain to the life-giving valley were black from head to toe. Except for their teeth."

"Bums. So what? They're all black up there. Like Faina."

"Doesn't it astonish you, Orlov, that people living so close to the sky should be as black as earth?"

"No, it doesn't."

"There you are, Orlov, I have to do it all myself," I said. "I haven't worked it out yet."

"You know something, Oktyabrina?" he says "I'd miss you – you and your revelations..."

He stopped talking, narrowed his eyes and stared over my shoulder. I turned round and there was Felix, standing in the dark corridor by the kitchen door, and we hadn't heard him. His red shirt was open over a round, yellow shoulder, his greasy black hair was thrown over the other shoulder, and he was tying it in complicated knots and staring sulkily at us.

Orlov started up. "Who the hell is that?" he muttered.

I was scared he'd been heard. I looked at Felix, who went shy and dropped his eyes.

"Come here, son," Orlov said. The boy didn't want to move – I could sense his back tense and his buttocks clench – but he didn't dare disobey and crept towards Orlov, who opened the table drawer and scooped out a handful of sticky sweets. Felix cupped his hands, but he didn't cup them tight enough and some fell on the floor. "I've dropped them!" he said, then picked them up and offered them round. Orlov smiled at him and shook his head. "Off to your room, son, the cartoons'll be on soon!" Felix nodded and went out.

"Behold the gently-reared son and the ardent bride..." said Orlov.

"Orlov!" I cried.

"Okay, you win," he sighed, "There's nothing up there!"

"I know," I sighed quietly too.

"Just the blackness of infinity!" he said malevolently.

I nodded.

"But you still can't prove it to me! I'm thirty years old – my life's not over yet!"

I said nothing.

"Answer me, Oktyabrina, answer me!" he screamed, carried away in a blinding rage.

At that I stood up, my brain flashing so violently that it scorched. "I've got an idea," I said.

"As if I didn't know!" Orlov wilted. "You never stop – ideas and miracles!"

"No miracles," I retorted. "Now I must think."

Orlov let me go, and I sat on my bed and jumped on the springs until they jingled, helping me to think about those unbelievably dark people.

When they found me in the blueness above the abyss, barely warm on the pale-pink rock, they spoke in guttural shrieks, and their dark, twisted tongues pierced the sky like knives. They shouted that they had found me and they were glad I was alive. They shouted and pointed at the sky, and I lifted my eyes to where they were pointing, and the sky looked down on us like strangers. I nodded to them that I understood, and I closed my eyes so the light wouldn't blind me. Then they bundled me up in a reeking goatskin which was dark and warm and smelled of goat, which feeds people with her body. And the goat carried me inside herself, rocking me to stop me crying, feeding me with the warmth of her belly and her living darkness, rocking me in herself to make me forget the unbearable blueness. And while the goat carried me inside her life-giving darkness, I carried in my own life-giving darkness my son. For there, where our dark-faced people carried me, the warmth of life ran dry – above was only the membrane of sky, and beyond it... And the son I bore in that life-giving warmth later pierced this membrane of sky... And all of us – the goat, and me, and the one who was inside me – were carried along by these dark-faced people! How many lives did these dark, stocky people carry from the deathly blue of the mountains to the life-giving darkness of the earthy valley...

It's not surprising they're so dark. If life was possible in that blueness, on those sharp, pale stones among the transparent winds and depths, the people would be bright, tall and transparent as angels, which don't exist – my Yura proved it – and which people have dreamed up in their longing for goodness, love and eternal life.

I bounced a bit more on the springs, and the jingling inspired true thoughts. All sorts of ideas flashed through my mind... Felix's red shirt, rippling and trembling like a living thing...

I didn't notice Faina standing there. I looked up absent-mindedly and there she was on my rug, all wet. She was wearing my dressing-gown which I'd put out to be washed. She was breathing heavily, and the dressing-gown was open on her breast.

"I went to the Moscow Soviet and the deputy said they'd be evicting you any day now!" she gasps.

"But he doesn't even know me!"

"He does now!" she says, giving a thin, scornful smile.

I ask her where the deputy is going to evict me to. She thinks. Her olive eyes search my room and come to rest on the shining face of my son.

"Up there!" she says with a terrible shriek, then cackles with laughter, jabbing her finger like a knife at the forehead of my star-pilot.

I freeze with terror as I look at this small, strong, dark woman who even at this distance smells of the sweat from my dressing-gown. She stands rubbing her wet, oily-black hair with a grey towel, and her lips shake as she speaks to me. Through the holes of my dressing-gown I can see her dark, buttery skin. A dark, swarthy body. The sour reek of goatskin flares in my memory...

"But people can't live up there!" I cry. "*You* know that!"

Ignoring me, she shouts, laughs and curses, jumping and dancing on my pink and white rug. Slapping her sides and squatting on the rug, she howls and shakes her hair over the floor: her deputy is in cahoots with her, and they plan to throw me into the blackness of infinity, the awful cosmic *kaput*, which has already burnt up the life of my star-boy, my son Gagarin.

I rise from my bed and raise my arm, signalling for her to be silent. She shrinks back. I speak clearly, to make sure that she understands: "You can't live up there. There's no life there. You *know* there isn't!"

She starts jumping up and down again, saying over and over: "Oh no, you're killing me! I'll die laughing!" But I raise my arm once more, and again she shrinks back in anticipation.

"Tell your deputy that Yura has proved there's life only on Earth," I tell her. "You can't throw me up there – it's against the law."

Faina tenses and looks warily at me. She bites her finger, and keeping her small worried eyes on me, she starts thinking. Then she says: "So stop telling Orlov not to marry me, or I'll have you evicted! I have a child!"

"Felix is not a child," I say mechanically, and raise my eyes in surprise at my words.

She opens her mouth ready to scream, but I point to the door and she is forced to leave. As soon as she is gone, I rush to the door and lock it. Then I clutch my head, and say: "My poor head! What have you thought up now? Quick, quick!"

Far away in the kitchen Faina was shouting, Orlov was shouting, and their shouts seemed to come from a distant, far-off world. I had to think on, the thought was so close, it teased my brain, then sank to the bottom. I paid no attention to Orlov and Faina hammering on my door – I mustn't be disturbed! I raised my hand, and even through the door they knew they had to be silent. I went on sitting there, deep in thought.

My son Gagarin floated up out of his sad weightlessness to the glass. He looked at me, my Star-boy, but he couldn't help me. I stroked the glass, hoping the warmth of my hand would pass through the impenetrable glass and warm the face of my space-boy.

I realised that Faina's story was a pack of lies. She would never have been allowed in to see the deputy, because she was a tramp. And she clearly didn't work at any newspaper either, because she was illiterate. I could understand why she lied, of course. Something had taken her from her people, or they'd banished her, and the fear of death had driven her to tramp the country and tell lies about friends and editorial offices in high places. Like everyone on this planet she wanted to live, but she didn't know how, so she stumbled around lying about deputies and *Komsomolskaya Pravda*. I remembered her sagging breasts in my dressing-gown. Maybe there's milk in those breasts, and this milk is seeking a little corner in which to give birth to and feed another tiny Felix. But over her head is nothing but blue sky.

I crept quietly to my son, and whispered to him: "You've punctured it, Yura. Forgive me, but everyone knows it was your ship that tore a hole in the sky and from it the poison of infinity leaked out. Faina wanted to throw me out – now it's dripping on her head, and the deputy's head, and every living head on the planet, and it's all your fault, Yura!"

And he barely manages to whisper: "I know Mother, but we agreed not to talk about it..."

I know we did, but oh, those pathetic breasts, which Faina tries to hide in my torn dressing-gown, and the infinity of space, which burns the milk in them even through it. Once again the sadness of eternity came over me, a sadness for all living things sentenced to destruction, thanks to my son, Yury Gagarin. It was at his head that Faina pointed, wishing me dead. My poor, poor Star-boy! They use you to frighten your mother, and she has nothing to say back to them!

I stopped bouncing on my bed and thinking, I just lay there and let the tears flow on to the pillow and my sadness become light and empty. And I said to myself: "Sleep until the new morning, and in the night tears of pity will flow and you may finally grasp the idea which flares then fades to the bottom of consciousness, lighting it with a searing flash, then dying in an explosion of heat. But at the centre of Earth blazes its unbearably hot heart, hotter even than Felix's red shirt. There at the life-giving centre of our Earth is life eternal, sheltering everything warm and trembling just like the goatskin did, soothing and rocking all living creatures! All of them alive, every one of them, just because she feels sorry for them!"

I jumped up from the bed, ran to Yura's portrait and tapped on the glass.

"What is it, Mother?" he said.

"Tell me, Yura, what do you know about the *returners?*"

He didn't speak for a long time, my Gagarin. I even thought he tried to look away from me, but he couldn't – he was bound by eternity.

"You know, Yura – the people who're looking for their way to the other side! Not like you, after all, you're a messenger from the heavens."

And again he didn't reply, the first star-man in the world.

"The ones who've found eternal life at the burning centre of Earth! That's why they're so dark, they're living at the source of life..."

"I... don't... know," he whispered barely audibly.

I knew he was lying – but why?

"Yura, it was you who let the poison seep through the wounds of the sky and doomed the Earth to a slow death! Don't turn away from me, I'm your mother!"

And my boy could no longer lie to me, and he said: "You need a ship."

"Yes, yes, Yura, a ship! Go on!"

"Make sure the engines are running and the nozzles blazing..." he whispered.

"But where is the ship?"

He wouldn't say any more. I pleaded with him, I fell on my knees, I raised my hands to him in the name of everything living, but he wouldn't tell me where the ship was, he just gleamed his white teeth at me in silence.

"Yura, Yura..." I passed the rose over his glass. "Destruction is dripping on to the Earth and the cosmos is devouring the last remaining drop of life in the universe!"

Only a quiet sigh came from the glass, and the dazzling silence of his smile.

I put the rose back in the water. And again I heard a sigh of relief, or did I imagine it? I gazed at my son's honest blue stare. He smiled at me through the glass. I pulled out the rose, and put it back again. A faint sigh came again from his bared smiling teeth.

Rose, rose, flame-red rose... I quietly pulled the flower from the narrow vase and stared into its depths, where the scrunched-up petals were so tightly swaddled they must be protecting its core, which contained the heat of life, the living, unfading flower.

I paced the floor. Bouncing on the bed no longer helped me, I needed movement, free and unencumbered movement. I strode around the room, begging the rose to help me. Obviously those dark people who rescued me from the blueness knew the path to the heart of Earth – they lived there. But how was I to find it? How could I reach every living thing sentenced to a slow death under a sky which at any minute will burst through and flood us with the soulless, airless, lightless space of the hungry cosmos?

I looked at Yura's portrait and gasped. It was dead, quite dead, flat as a newspaper photo, framed in glass! As though he was no longer my son! Without the rose, fragment of the magma, hot, blazing red, like Felix's shirt, he no longer had the strength to live.

"You knew!" I shout at him.

He knew, he knew. He'd been nourished by a drop of magma which happened to land here on Earth – he lived on it, and he said nothing to the rest of us!

I go numb with anger. "You care only about your life! The world's groaning in a slow death, but you're all right, you got through! You're no son of mine! I renounce you, Gagarin!"

I grab the glass, ringing with pain, and hurl it to the floor, stamping it into stardust, just as he deserves.

And the rose? How will it show us the way to salvation? Rose, red as blood, drop of the life-giving magma, distant relative of Felix's shirt... Carmen, shirt... Rose plus Felix, Felix plus shirt, rose plus Felix – join them together and they make a ship! The good ship *Carmen*! Engines running, nozzles blazing! We'll go down, down to the source of eternal life! How good! How simple! Rose plus Felix!

I have to keep my wits about me so as not to frighten the others. I take the rose and stare fearlessly around my room. Here it was that I passed my life, here I cherished memories of my hero, here I stamped his face into stardust, and from here I shall lead all living things to the centre of Earth and eternal life, where no drop of heavenly eternity will fall on us.

I go to the kitchen. Orlov gives a little sigh.

"Watch out!" I say.

"Oktyabrina!" he shouts.

I raise my hand. But Orlov shouts over it: "Please, Oktyabrina, I'm begging you!"

"Get ready, everyone! We're going under the Earth!" I shout.

Faina starts guffawing. Suddenly out of the blue Orlov yells at her: "Hold your tongue, that's my mother!"

I nod, he understands – yes, I'm everyone's mother now! I'm mother to all the people I'm going to save and lead to the source of all life. The tears are pouring down Orlov's cheeks. I speak harshly: "Time's running out, Orlov! Get ready! The engines are running, the nozzles are blazing!"

"Tie her down, Yura, tie her down!" shrieks Faina.

I turn abruptly to Felix. He stands with his face lifted to mine, squeezing my noodles in his hands. His hair, flowing like water-weed, circles his puffy face, his shivering collar-bones, his chest and his ribs, but his olive eyes are sharp and attentive. Because this boy is one of the returners, he knows that he is our ship. I thrust the rose at him from behind my back and shout: "Here Carmen, take the rose!"

At that moment the sharp stem of the rose pierces his heart and starts to grow. At that moment Felix's magmatic shirt blazes and merges with the magmatic rose. At that moment his magmatic chest reveals its red, hot interior. And at that moment it turns into a ship. In a loud voice I start counting: "One! Two!..."

At the count of three everyone grabs Felix because his nozzles were blazing and his motors were roaring. He starts to bore his way into the Earth, and as I shout "Three!" we all throw ourselves at him and grab him, and the Earth finally opens herself up to us with a groan. And then we descend with frantic haste to its heart, as it blazes joyfully ahead of us. And our good ship *Carmen* is scorched in the friction, but we are already so close, so close, so close...

And the Earth closes above our heads, sheltering us forever from death, sadness and the terror of infinity...

Diamonds and Irons

The Jewish Rosenfelds, six to eight families, lived in Magadan. They liked it, with clenched hearts. Far away in the distance floated Israel, sad as Turkish delight, looking at them across the world with heavy lids and calling to its children. The Rosenfelds, hearts clenched, said: "Let us go, so our children will have a homeland, and the children of their children will never know there is on earth a foreign land!"

The older Jews wept, not understanding why Magadan was a foreign land. Magadan is a hard, barren place, but the Jews had all been born there, as had their parents. Not one of them was born in Israel, and they were afraid. But they had to go, they had to bear children in Israel – one, two, three times. "See that curly-haired child running on golden legs, his little heart is light and the sweet breeze of childhood is in his soul," people would say. "This child knows no other land, this child is from here – rejoice!"

Wanting to experience this extraordinary joy, the Rosenfelds sold their flats, and while they were waiting to be allowed to leave they all moved into the room of their nephew, Alik Rosenfeld. It was cramped there, but this scattered family, the gaps between them more like cold expanses, was astonished to find they didn't mind this extreme intimacy, but found themselves clinging closer together. And unlike the Russian working class, they had all had large flats before. Say what you like, the Jews know how to live! As they clung together in Alik's one-room shell, not understanding why they didn't get angry with one another, they remembered that people had lived like this in ancient times, before their wanderings twanged the string of that dark, patriarchal time.

In the evenings, the old people would gather by the window and talk together in whispers. Would there be grief? No more than cunning. And joy? No less than peace. When they looked around them in dark Magadan it was impossible to see a better fate, just the same lives flickering through the hush of the winter evening. The same, but not the same. It was for others to endure this hated land to the death, and to know their life was a long feat of endurance.

The old people looked through the window at the blue snow and sighed quietly, remembering the creaking deer-skin boots of their childhood. They asked each other if they would be able to learn the dark, chocolate-like language of Hebrew, and if so, what would become of the language they spoke now, privately whispering to one another in "the mother tongue." The old people felt awkward speaking their language, which was now a foreign language, so they kept their peace and looked out of the window at the shining blue snow, wondering where the footprints of the little reindeer boots had gone.

The virgin snow shone severe and regal as the young people dreamed in the kitchen. Alik Rosenfeld, a thin, pasty-faced young man who painted water-colours of flowers, listened to his heart thumping as he imagined the pictures he would paint in Israel. The others too had their dreams, the girls of drumrolls and bathing-suits, the boys of fat bags of money and serious talk in the evenings when the sun flooded the sky of Israel with fire. The little ones romping at their feet dreamed of flying in an aeroplane.

Having sold their flats, the Rosenfelds decided to use the money to buy diamonds from the jeweller's shop and to take the hard, mean gems with them to Israel, so that this southern land might know how unbearably the Magadan snow sparkled at night. The Jews had to employ cunning, of course, since the USSR doesn't allow diamonds to be taken out of the country. You can be France for all the USSR cares, it's not allowed – and that's that! It's all so confusing. Say you're a collector, you go into a shop, a diamond takes your fancy and you buy it with your own money, not the USSR's. The USSR says nothing while you're buying it, as though it had a mouth full of water, but try taking it abroad and they'll yell that it's Soviet property, as if they'd bought it themselves! What a mess. No honest person can make head or tail of it – when they see the dangerous flash of the jewels they just spit and walk on. Don't even consider it, you'd be mad. But if they're the USSR's property, what's it putting its own goods on sale for? To be worn, or what? It's weird. Never mind, don't think about it.

So our Jews decided to be cunning. It wasn't clear how they would outwit the USSR, which wasn't human after all, and didn't seem alive until those four letters crushed you so your ribs cracked. But our Jews had to be cunning, whispering together and brushing each other with their long noses as they worked out what to do if they got caught with their diamonds. You could understand their thinking. The reason these little gems are so hard is that they're worth an extraordinary amount of money, and this is very convenient – why drag around bags stuffed with greasy notes when you can carry a couple of stones and know they mean cash! Especially if you're flying abroad, and don't like the idea of lugging all your bags on to the plane.

So they agreed on the most suitable type of stone, and so that the USSR wouldn't kick up a fuss they decided to hide them in the most private parts of their body. (Since

the USSR has no body, or anything else you can understand, it knows nothing about people's private parts.)
They appealed to the girls, who blushingly agreed, then set
off for the jewellery store. At first they sensibly decided to
send only a couple of the most cunning Rosenfelds to
select the hardest, most sparkling stones, but in the end
those who dreamed of flying on a plane were joined by
the entire assembly of Jews, even the very youngest.

They all poured in. The Jewish girls wandered through
the store, happily leaning their flower-like faces over the
flower brooches, which tremblingly offered themselves to
the pretty girls on the other side of the glass. But they
couldn't flirt for long before they were all herded off to
the diamond department, where the diamonds lay gleaming like bullets on their black velvet. Hopeless and
withdrawn, not dreaming of an owner, hostages to the
USSR which gave them nothing to hope for, the diamonds
were mean and lonely, and now these shouting, excited
Jews were gazing at them with their brown eyes. Their life
was virginally brief – straight from the factory to their
new owners. How much light they concealed, blinding the
Rosenfelds' warm eyes through the glass – as if to say,
we're yours!

The Rosenfelds bought two rings and a pair of ear-
rings, four diamonds in all, not including the diamond
chips surrounding each stone. They were served by the
entire sales staff. The distracted manager hovered puncti-
liously around his wealthy customers, and the neat, bright-
eyed sales girl displayed the stones on her fingers and her
small ears, setting off their shine to the best advantage.
Never before had our Jews enjoyed such attention,
although they knew shop assistants over there were like
this. They even experimented with making a nuisance of
themselves, and demanded a new box for the stones. The
neat sales girl smiled with calm eyes, the manager hovered
gracefully.

Back at home, each took turns tentatively touching the

Diamonds and Irons

diamonds. Allowed to try them on, the girls imperceptibly changed and became subtly prettier, while the others waved their arms and whooped with delight. Thus skinny, whey-faced Alik fell hopelessly in love with lazy Masha, when the gleam of the stones illuminated her for him with a momentary and terrible clarity. Not daring to lift his eyes to her face, he told her that he would buy stones for her like these in Jerusalem, and she shrugged her shoulders. The little ones were allowed to wear the diamonds too, for the sake of fairness. They called them plane headlamps. The others shouted that a plane had searchlights, not headlamps, and the little ones were forced to give the diamonds back. After this it was decided to put the stones away safely until it was time for them to board the plane.

There were a great many Rosenfelds. The larger part of them were highly strung, prone to exhaust themselves with shouting and stormy gestures. Words poured from them faster than thoughts, and this dense stream of emotions sometimes obliterated the sense of their words. Such people might easily talk about the stones. They decided that only old Isaiah should know where they were, and that everyone would leave the flat while he calmly looked for somewhere to hide them. The Rosenfelds went out on to the street and looked up at the window. But clever Isaiah had switched off the light. The Rosenfelds sighed, but they knew it had to be that way. Old Isaiah went to the bathroom, lifted a tile from the floor, laid the stones beneath it, then replaced the tile and scrubbed the floor. After this he switched the light back on, and the Rosenfelds knew the stones were hidden.

It was unusually quiet that evening. Four powerful new strangers gleamed in the small, crowded flat. Who were the strangers? What would they bring to the Rosenfeld clan? Happiness. A quiet happiness, and a stormy happiness. You name it, they brought it. To each his own. That's the way happiness is, different for everyone.

The young people felt shy. The older ones sat quietly by the window. The little ones were hardly naughty at all. Smiling furtively at one another, the Rosenfelds went off to wash in the kitchen and were in bed early.

Weep, children of Israel, weep, ye Jews! At dawn the bolt clicked metallically, and this click betrayed them. It was always a traitor, it knew always that it would betray them, waiting for the right time, clicking like a cocked pistol and opening the gates of weeping.

At dawn, when sleep is most necessary, the lock clicked drily, the door swung open, and in swept a draft and four men. The moment the traitor clicked, the Rosenfelds simultaneously opened their eyes in response to the sound, holding their breath in the faint hope that the Rosenfelds didn't exist, never had, never would, not in this flat or anywhere else – on no corner of the Earth, circling in the constellations of the cosmic abyss, were the Rosenfelds to be found! Haven't seen them, don't know where they are! Their Doba just received greetings from you-know-who in Odessa. What joy! God grant Doba happiness! Yet Doba is nowhere. The Rosenfelds have gone. The Earth circles in the cosmic abyss, but the Rosenfelds aren't here!

Then some of the little ones wet their beds, and not only the Rosenfelds heard them, but the four strangers too. They waited until the noise had stopped – they mustn't embarrass the little ones, or it might make them incontinent – then they switched on the light. "Here they are!" they said.

The four were in civilian clothes, straight as letters of the alphabet. Under their feet, wherever they trod, shone black eyes, alive and waiting.

"Rosenfelds, tell us where the diamonds are!" said the four. The Rosenfelds turned instinctively away from Isaiah.

"Okay, we'll find them ourselves," the four said.

They rampaged through the flat, like a hungry man

devouring a chicken.

"Well?" they said to the Rosenfelds after they had rampaged. One of them had a scraggy little neck and big eyes; he seemed unbearably awkward and was evidently new, and looked as though he might at any minute burst into sobs and kill someone.

"We'll get them, d'you hear – we'll torture you!" said the four. "We'll put the iron to you, every single one of you!" The new one's upper lip was covered in a thick sweat.

The Rosenfelds were then gagged, which was why they did not cry out while they were being ironed. The little ones assumed it was just something you had to do, like having your inoculations at nursery-school, and they all lined up, whining a bit and pulling up their little shirts. The new one would occasionally step over to one of the little ones and give him a smack. He did so carefully, and his eyes, fixed on those of the chosen one, were white, and his face flashed with madness.

The Jews started to give off a roasting smell. One of the four threw up. From the depths of the Rosenfelds came a moaning sound, like a distant song, or a heavy branch in the summer heat, or the word "Jerusalem". The new one suddenly stood still, inclined his head tensely, and fell to the ground with a sigh. But the Rosenfelds did not think of singing, they were mortally afraid. They looked timidly at old Isaiah, hoping he would say where the diamonds were, but Isaiah ostentatiously looked ahead, through the irons, the Rosenfelds and the wall into the cosmic abyss, to where the Rosenfelds would depart after squandering their time on the green glades of this world.

"Come here, Jew!" they called to Isaiah.

Isaiah went.

The man quietly placed the iron on Isaiah's hollow stomach and looked anxiously into his eyes. Isaiah knew the man was afraid he might die. But Isaiah knew he would not die. It had happened before and he had not died. In the German concentration camp he had not died. In the Soviet concentration camp he had not died. Now he would not die. When would he die? Isaiah decided to ask himself if he might die. No, he would not die. In Isaiah's stomach, just above his intestines and near his chest, lived something that moaned and trembled. This was the moaning sound they had heard. The new one had thought it was a song, and had collapsed senseless. But it wasn't a song, it was the inner workings of Isaiah and all the Rosenfelds. The Rosenfelds did not have such a fine sense of personal property as the four, they simply clung to the string of life, moaning from eternal danger. Isaiah longed to scream and weep, but he was too old and no longer had the strength. He had wept in the German concentration camp, he had wept in the Soviet concentration camp. If he wept here, with the iron on his stomach, it would be from his utter powerlessness to show that he, Isaiah, wanted to live.

"... diamonds?!!"

Isaiah said they were under a tile in the bathroom.

"Why didn't you tell us, Jew?"

Isaiah hadn't deliberately kept silent, he had just forgotten about the stones the moment he heard the treacherous click. If they had said to him: "Isaiah, hand over your filthy stones!" he would have done so at once, but he could not because something incomparably more important had happened, which has been happening for hundreds of centuries: he had been reminded.

Isaiah secretly reproached God with just one thing: "Why didst Thou grant the Jews the same love of life as other innocent people?"

But because Isaiah's reproach was secret, God did not hear.

In the plane the Rosenfelds looked around them curiously. They loved it. The little ones pressed the buttons, and smart young men and women came up, laughter dancing in their eyes, murmuring kindly and smiling at the little ones with their clean teeth. The little ones' mouths hung open with delight. The older ones, who had the window-seats, put rugs over their knees and pillows at their heads. They liked these comforts, and they liked flying through the blue and white sky, and though they were afraid of flying they were too comfortable with their pillows and rugs to admit it. The young people drank their drinks and pretended they had been flying all their life. The red triangles on their stomachs would always be brown now, and no longer hurt.

Old Isaiah slowly drank his lemonade. He sat in the tail of the aircraft and looked at the back of the Rosenfelds' curly heads. The iron had scorched his departure from Magadan, but after the pain eased it turned out that Magadan still had a place in the old Jew's memory. The snow, the smell, a snatch of sound...

But Isaiah was not thinking about this now. He wanted to know why Jews had yet again resorted to cunning and pretended to be like everyone else. Why did they build the state of Israel and rush there from all parts of the world? Just so they could utter that awkward foreign phrase "my country"? Isaiah wondered if the Rosenfelds had brought enough coats with them, and if the little ones had warm cardigans. Maybe they had, maybe they hadn't. Isaiah was old, and his thoughts were confused. There was just one thing he didn't want to think about, and that was when they would start torturing the Jews in Israel. He knew it wouldn't be long. But he didn't want to think about it now, because he liked living too much.

The plane carried the Jews on and on. The Jews flew through the blue sky. The USSR looked up to the blue sky and saw the white stripe, and the diamonds returned to their black velvet in the shop.

The Wind from the Suburbs

Green animal faces peer out, clustering every so often around the shoulders of the people they especially desire. Their hot dull muzzles are wrenched open by monstrous roars, which make us maliciously want to stand before them. They gaze at us, inexpressibly gold, with their intelligent blue eyes. From their faces everything hangs and pours. Where ours are smooth and silky, theirs are rough and craggy. Where we are hot and tight, they are loose and cool. Where our youth dances, their old age crashes about them – and this is not a venerable old age, oh no, for they are beautiful monsters. They pity us for wishing them dead. Slobbering, they look at us with their gold-blue eyes, while our blood boils inside us with war, war, war. And for us there is no going back.

That winter, not this one, in the middle of a wet January day which ploughed the snowy water deep beneath our feet, when people waded higgledy-piggledy up to their waists, when Moscow was tear-streaked with lights, and Caucasian banquets gleamed in smart restaurants and on our tablecloths. That winter, drunken old women sprawled around, begging wasn't forbidden, and one-legged young men cast brazen eyes at our feet as the hand clumsily threw a kopeck at their eyes. That winter, no one in the city had money and everyone was young. That winter there was communism – the kingdom of the identically poor, light as air in their unexpected youth. All could touch the ground, and people threw themselves down so the water could wash their chests. That winter, as Russians stretched themselves from sleep, we expected war and heaven and help from the Americans, everyone loved Lithuania, the Caucasus wasn't burning, Asia didn't lap at our feet, the republics hadn't split off, and young men stood on the corner of windy Mayakovsky Square selling things.

Seeing someone I recognise there, I stop out of curiosity – although the lads standing around there are people you'd normally avoid. Assuming I am someone's girl-friend, they politely move aside. They're large and sweaty with wine, covered with the long wet winds off Gorky Street.

The beefy booksellers stand there in their wet, heavy clothes as I say to my acquaintance: "Hi there, Dima!"

"Wanna buy a book?" Dima grins.

I jump, then the singer in me starts chatting to these young masters of the book, talking to each of them but not daring to look directly at dark young Dima, just turning my face slightly towards him and a bit of my shoulders, as though to catch the reflection from his face and some of his warmth with my chest. The others can see at once that I love Dima, even on this wet, windy darkening street corner, which slips away and falls down the steps in the steamy draft of the underground entrance.

On a little red granite ledge on their wretched slipping-away corner, the boys have laid out golden books so they can buy wine and get drunk. My entreaties beat at their wet overcoats, and they move aside to let me in, huge and angry with Dima for his coldness to me.

It's not that I don't love Dima, I just don't know him. I sing for them because I want to be with them, out of curiosity or just a whim perhaps. Because we hardly know each other, this odd-faced lad dare not call my bluff, he just wrinkles his smooth forehead. He hardly knows me enough to say a word, in fact, especially as I'm a well-known singer, like Edith Piaf or Elena Obraztsova, with my name, Anna Ivanova, on that poster up there.

He's upset of course, because his mates, like me, turn away from him – the chosen one, set apart from the rest, pursued by a girl he doesn't love. Maybe she has been following him around not daring to speak to him, and he has told her to stop but she can't. So I come on even stronger, surreptitiously clinging to him and breathing: "Why didn't you phone?"

Why do I badger the boy? He doesn't even know my number. I suppose I got carried away. Then he slowly swings his body towards me, like the globe, peers keenly at me with his dark, inquisitive, odd-shaped little eyes and waits for what will happen next. I speak quietly to him. Realising that the others can't hear, he lets me know with his rough soul that they will pick up my every word and movement. But I want nothing from them, it's just the eternal, impossible, capricious desire to see what people are selling on the other side of the street – a cake with a bite out of it? A comb? Half a make-up mirror?

I really should have left it there, with the virginally downcast faces of Dima's comrades standing loveless in the wind, because there's only one of them who means trouble, and that's a little street-kid amongst all those husky, tall, slow-moving lads. This kid is definitely on the racket, and I should have left it at that. But no, they discreetly move further away from me, and from the Racket too, ducking and weaving around their legs. Still they keep moving away, and I know I should just leave, but I come on even stronger so they'll trust me and stop moving away from me, and I won't have to duck and weave like the Racket. I'm scared of losing them!

As I stumble unthinkingly off the wet street into this group of young strangers, I mock love to the wind. They listen, then they silently stand aside, squeezing me in with their tall shoulders like a wounded comrade before the firing squad. Simple-hearted and sharp-eyed, what if they see I'm bluffing? Why do they sadly welcome me into their warm circle and listen to me with lowered eyes? They could have coldly watched me capering before them in the wind and turned away with bored faces, talking amongst themselves quietly but ever more loudly, ignoring me like waiters. But they don't, for they are mothers' boys. Instead they share their wine with me, and we swig down the bitter red mouthfuls together. God is good!

Things get even funnier. It turns out that both ginger-haired Tolyan and Alyosha with the fur hat live with their mothers. What brings these two boys here, so different yet so similar? They should be at home with their mothers, two women living in different parts of the city, instead of standing here selling books. It makes you weep, they're so big and trusting, freezing to death without their poor mums. Now Dima's softly taking my hand, and there's another tall one too, also nice-looking, his face all angry and rough, because he's hopelessly married so he hasn't really got a mum. Shivering at our feet is the Racket, a little ruffian from Matveevka, who dreamed up his name, lovely as a motorbike, to shock the big mothers' boys.

Passers-by hold out their hands and we place golden books in them. Then, whirling around us, all of a sudden appear shreds and tatters from a garden which is being torn up somewhere, and branches flowering with milk and hazy green confusion. The danger lasts only for a second, as we stand there even straighter and redder-cheeked, imagining our mothers weeping and bending over our little heads and stroking our hair. Here's ginger-haired Tolyan, big as the sun – his mum must see how funny and precious he is, and how he can never get anything right. He says: "Look at that idiot standing there staring at the books, he doesn't understand a thing!"

Gentle, lovely Tolyan left school at thirteen and has books about rocket engines. Alyosha opposite, sly, moody and gentle, wants to run away from people, which makes him cling to them even more. He has shiny, clever books. They all have clever books except Tolyan, and they all

drink away their money together. They don't give it to
their mothers, they spill it. Even angry John-with-no-name,
older than the rest because he's married, organises his
hopeless little books to make them more appealing. Dima
with his screwed-up eyes, his swagger and some special
thought on his flat, dark face, scares off outsiders with his
street talk and defends the others because he's their leader.
He organises them, like they organise each other and clink
their glasses together.

Mothers hurry past with their little boys, who turn
back their meek, pale faces and stretch out their hands,
pleading with their eyes: "Please Mum, Russian fairy-tales!"

"Come on, Alyosha, we're in a hurry!"

Suddenly realising he's alone, the Racket bends down,
lunges at our legs as though taking a bow and pounces on
ginger-haired Tolyan. Angry and embarrassed, as though
kidding around, he punches Tolyan painfully in the ribs,
then jumps back, waiting to see if the others will punch
him. They don't. Wounded, Tolyan stands there open-faced
and alone, everything sweet and precious torn from his
chest, an ugly lad with a fat red face. The others overcome
their dislike of his humiliation and reach out to pour him
wine, as the tears stream down Tolyan's pocked face, and
we are all brothers again and the Racket's a jackal.

Suddenly, my God, more shreds and tatters from the
seething garden whirl past us and on.

"What was that?" says ginger-haired Tolyan. "It's
choking me!"

"It's bad," pipes up gentle Alyosha.

"It'll get us!" Dima says. John grinds his teeth.

Then Alyosha shouts out to a Georgian man passing
by: "Hey, mister, buy a book!"

The Georgian starts, understands, and flashes his
spectacles, and the more he roars the louder we laugh.
Standing on tiptoe and throwing himself into a Georgian
dance, as though to escape this cursed Russian land, the
man flings up his arms to his beloved mountains, and
dollars fan out in his dark fingers ("A million!"), and we

all die laughing, because he's so hopelessly black and our funny Alyosha is so undoubtedly, unquestionably Russian. The horse-eyed Caucasus spreads wide its legs, shouting: "I'll kill my Russian brothers!" I fall on Dima howling, and the Racket crows triumphantly at our feet, because his dream has finally come true and we have insulted someone.

Then some people come up with faces like lakes. They look at the books, we look at the lakes, they move off. There follow a few sad moments and the plain misery of cold feet. Time passes, I feel something funny tickle the bridge of my nose and I brush it off. Insistent as a puppy's breath, it tickles my nose again and I rub it, only to discover it's someone's cold lips, and it's Alyosha telling me something, and I've been listening to him all along, deep in my own thoughts. We all laugh again, then we drink. The jackal lunges again, this time at Dima. He kicks him – in the backside, though we couldn't have seen it – and Dima stoops over and kicks the jackal, who rolls away yelping, and I announce: "Hey boys, I'm a singer!"

A clear voice above me instantly responds: "We know you are, Anna Ivanovna!"

We laugh again, because they all know I'm Anna Ivanova, not Ivanovna, and I point at the poster fluttering by the underground entrance. Following my finger, the jackal jumps up, rips the poster down and tears it up, looking around him with the vengeful grin of a homeless orphan. At this all the brothers stand up as one and shout: "That's it, now you've blown it!"

I say: "Don't worry boys, let's spit instead!"

So we spit three times, as though at the devil, and the jackal disappears. It's a good thing the jackal existed, because it means we can spit at him and he disappears. We stand drinking in silence. John says he's fed-up because he got married too young and has children, and it's true, he does look fed-up. Then Dima looks at me, something flickers over his swarthy face, his dark, screwed-up eyes examine me closely, and the words he speaks seem full of the sound y. It's funny, and we kiss. We all clink glasses again and drink. Tolyan, dead drunk now, breaks into a folk song, and in that deafening moment I look upwards to avoid the noisy song, and my eyes blaze with such ferocity that suddenly I'm singing too and the tears are pouring down my hot cheeks. My god, what's wrong with me! What is this golden blue flooding my eyes! It's lucky the jackal was around – I was worried the little ruffian might rough us up, when I could have lifted my eyes and they would have blazed with this ruthless, inhuman implacability. Yes, the blue and the gold have been here all along, and they are pitiless. The dead are fallen, our books are spread out, their colours bleeding away as timid hands touch them, and I stumble along clutching at Dima's shadow. Dima the leader, Dima the boss, so blow me down if I didn't move in with him, oh the pain, the gold and the blue flooding my eyes, which I love to close when Dima loves me, so while he's loving me I can kiss the blue and the gold which splashed into them outside the underground station that winter.

I love Dima climbing on top of me in the blizzard, because then I can be alone with my beloved gold and my flattering blue, secret brothers of the same womb. I embrace them and shall never part from them, because we three are forever in the same womb: me, bold brother gold, quiet brother blue, all sharing the same cord. This is what I think while Dima climbs on top of me and loves me. Nobody knows what I am thinking. I used to think every couple in the world was like this, men climbing on top of women, women kissing their own eyes.

That winter I say: "We need to be comfortable, Dima, like other people – soft things, with deep round places to dive into like nests, vases gleaming on the window-sill so when the blizzard's blowing outside, the shining snow will kiss their sides. I love blizzards and carpets, and lots, lots more. You know the sort of place a woman needs. A woman's home needs lots of useful, beautiful things in it."

As I listen to the storm he listens to me, tilting his head to catch everything I say, then he looks up at me, and something flickers over his face as he says: "I'll fix it."

I nod. I don't give a damn what our flat's like, I just know that's what people want. "I'll fix it," he says, and the strange *y* sound rings even louder in my ears.

He brings back outlandish objects, and it would have scared me if I cared. He arranges them in the room, and they give off a huge, muted *y* in the twilight. His face is flickering, something is happening. I touch his cheeks and stroke them, and he smiles and looks away. At that moment a bubble which he has stuck to the radiator starts to swell up, and through its yellow murk I see something gurgling and fermenting inside. I squat gloomily on the floor for ages watching the bubble stirring. It is tight and warm, fed by the warmth of the radiator. Dima loves it. "It's you and me!" he says.

Winter dies, then storms again, dies, storms. I am unaware of standing all this time by the window watching for the blizzard, I think – I am just watching the bubble. It trebles in size, swaying in the low mysterious currents which follow our movements. It's funny. I step around it to the window, waiting for the storm, and it turns to follow me as though it too wants to be near the storm.

One day Dima says: "Let's prick it!"

I hear the *y* flash, piercing the sky, as he bursts the bubble and some thick yellow stuff oozes out. He pours it into two mugs, sticks up the hole with his spit and gives one mug to me. It smells of nothing, just stares at me from the mug. He silently drinks his and a smoky distant light plays over his face. Bewitched, I gulp mine down too.

Then I yell: "It's all a crazy mistake! You're not Dima at all, you're dark, treacherous Dyrdybaev!"

Squatting down, Dyrdybaev slaps his ribs in noiseless laughter. Smoky-green in the stars, *y* roars victory from my chest to the sky as the bubble stuff spreads and becomes sticky, and I am overwhelmed by mortal sadness.

Extricating myself from Dyrdybaev's sticky paws, I point my finger menacingly at him: "Watch out, Dyrdybaev, the unearthly garden will put its hooks into you! You'll lie there begging it for water and burning in torment!"

And he squats there silently laughing, slapping his sides with joy.

Heal my poor body, Alyosha, it's in a fever, bite it in the leg. It's me, Anna Ivanova. Remember when we all froze to death on the street corner that winter? Falling, swooning, dying? Remember me coming up to you and you let me in? I blew it, Alyosha, I didn't see you and grabbed the wrong one by mistake. Gardens rolled over me, bullets whistled, enemies burned my eyes, stuff like that. There was booze too, but that's okay. I don't know how I fell in with you lot, something led me to you, everything rolling around, people getting killed, winter, the weeping lights of Moscow, everything new, foreign words, Coke, Pepsi, nowhere to go, so I fell in with you lot, laughing, golden Alyosha, give me hope, Alyosha, do you remember me, Alyosha? Cooee, Alyosha! Don't be like that, we can make it. The moment you say yes, I'll be right over. "Tra-la-la!" – or is it the other way round?

"Hallo, is that you Alyosha?"

"Hello, A-a-anna Ivan-oh-my-god-ovna."

"Alyosha, I'm in one of my moods. Can I see you?"

"Oo... I... er... um..."

"I'm on my way, it's me, Ivanova!"

Heal me, cure my fever! What's that dark woolly bird lying on your chest with its feathers ruffled? Is that its shadow on your brows and lashes? Can I touch it? Your neck, your shoulders, the strong, even warmth of your life, Alyosha, your golden hair, I daren't speak of your eyes, your face is golden and dangerous, your body is armoured in young beauty, you're armoured, Alyosha, invisible. Put on your coat, city child, cool and loving. Do you know Siberia? They don't have snow there like your snow here. Here it chills your bones and makes you sad. There in blue Siberia, with its swamps and forests, clear eyes can make out a dairy farm, a path to the village, milkmaids carrying churns full of milk. The air is so clean there's no need for

The Wind from the Suburbs

lids so they can see the milk. Who can see it? The forest creatures, that's who, with their golden eyes. A playful creature with high cheek-bones and tasselled ears, a sulky, golden animal living in her clear forest home with her fluffy humility and her cruel heart, she spatters the snow with blood, pricks up her ears and starts as snowflakes scatter from the branches. She shakes her tasselled ears, a freckled, gingery, lynx-like creature.

Only she knows that she is alone, and they torment her, not on purpose of course, but they all live together and she is alone. She peeps out to see how they live, and here comes Anna Ivanova the milkmaid, carrying milk with no lid. There's not much to say now about Anna Ivanova, it's all in the past, a woman who wears warm trousers to keep her ovaries warm, husband at home drinking all day, fights over the housekeeping, numb fingers, heavy body, carrying milk to the village with no lid, but it's so clean here, so clear, white and silent, just the snow-dust circling and sparkling in the air as it drifts off the branches with a secret snowy thud. Anna carries the milk, white as snow, but warm and living, and her felt boots squeak as she walks. Whenever she passes this spot here she looks at the path with alarm, and notices the snow beside it turning blue and shadows spreading from the bushes. Reach home before dark and there's nothing to worry about. The forest is silent, that's our village over there. What do you take me for? I'm not scared, just step on it, the other women will laugh when I tell them, I can see the smoke, our houses are strong, she's back, it's me, I'm back!

As Ivanova carries her open churn, the snow squeaking under her tread, she thinks about the pig and the firewood, knowing nothing of the wild, sullen passion she has lit in the lonely creature, or the pitch of despair it has now reached. The creature struggles, but she can no longer stop herself – she creeps down this path every day, looking with tears and horror at the red-cheeked woman. Ivanova feels something, a warm, faint sob brushes her cheek, but she thinks it's only the cold and stamps her feet as she hurries on to the village. The little cat is alone in the darkening forest, alone with her insatiable sadness in her cool native forest. She squirms, unaware that she is doing wrong, for she is only an animal. She bites herself all over to drive away the vision of the woman, but what can she do, she is in its power. The snow cools her fluffy white stomach as she creeps forward in a fever, squirming and mewing, scratching the air with her outstretched claws. Snow scatters from the branches above her, but it signifies nothing, it just happens. Everything in the world is bright except the creature. She has no choice, she cannot wait. The moment has come, Alyosha, she is driven to the limit. Burning in the torment of her greed, she braces herself as the longed-for Ivanova floats through the snow-drifts bearing milk which gently splashes over the edges, bright as a cow, peace, a world without passion.

Ivanova has already reached the pine copse, where she always feels something tickling her through the bushes. In this shadowy place she slows down, and it's then that the creature rears up with a sob to embrace the chest of the beautiful one. Hard-working Ivanova is not a passionate woman. She lifts up her childish eyes and the gold and blue instantly sizzles them up. She tries to cry out, but her throat is slit open. Soaking and staggering, nightmarishly understanding everything, she throws out her arms to catch the gold and blue (how did I live without you, my gold and my blue!), but she clutches only the bright, bright air (for her fingers are stiffened with toil), and so blazing Ivanova staggers and stumbles, her slit-open throat gasping for air, and even the smallest twigs and branches are bright. The bright lynx, her crooked cheekbones gleaming gold in the bright sun, neatly laps the milk from the churn, lifting her freckled nose to the milky trickle and tilting her ears towards Ivanova, red, thirsty and feverish as she smokily staggers from this bright world, dappling the plumes of the bright falcon as he waits for her to depart.

The lynx grows bright as Ivanova grows dark, that's how it is, Alyosha! Ahead stand twenty men, twenty of the village's finest. They have seen everything, and now they start yelling, sharpening their knives and oiling their rifles. The dogs go crazy. The crazy blokes kick their crazy dogs. Robbed of their Ivanova, they look with hatred at their wives. Oblivious to them, the bright lynx plays in a snow-drift, she sniffs the air, she loves life, she chases a rabbit in the snow, she is a rabbit. But the twenty crazed men's blood boils when they see Ivanova on the ground. Poor men, they should have cooled down and realised that since one is gone and will not return they might as well leave the other alone. But no, Alyosha, they chase the animal and fire at her again and again, wanting to hear her death cry, trembling with desire, not knowing what to do with her, bearing down on her fluffy white chest and asking one another if their beautiful creature is dead.

The snow squeaks as they stamp around her, shouting in the silence of the bright twilit forest and rushing about in a fever. From that moment they abandon their wives and hit the drink, and at night, God help them, through the tears in their icy gold eyes they see blueness and milk. They could have loaded a rifle with sleeping pellets, aimed it at the untameable creature, kissed her all over while she slept, then run away, so when she awoke she'd dash about in a frenzy. Give her back what started it, instead of twenty men crashing around like fools – twenty manly breasts to kill one fluffy red passion.

Everyone in Belyaevo knows that if there had been no milk little Alyosha would have died. He comes into the world with his cupid mouth, and they all know he needs milk. That's how they save him. The neighbours anxiously bring warmed bottles saying, here's milk for your little one – add a drop of sugar and he'll think it's breast-milk. Look, he's drinking! Alyosha's mum leans over and watches him. He drinks. Her breast swells. It's winter. She has a fever. He has milk. The world is bright and ticking. Nobody goes out. Everyone stays in. A radio plays behind the wall. People are home after work, waiting for their next day off.

Alyosha's mother – our flat's high up, the wind blows at the windows – weakly holds the baby in her weak arms then drops him, like most Russian children are dropped to their grannies or to children's homes. Clutching their heads the mothers look out of the windows as Moscow's suburbs turn to evening and the news comes on the radio on the other side of the wall. Her fluffy head spins, curls stick to her damp temples, tears of lights pour down, taxis pass, call Volgograd to see how Alyosha is, but keep her salty golden eyes fixed on the lights below, such youth in my breast, the milk not for my boy, righteous God, Komsomol honour, cooee, help Mayday! It's still winter, night-time in the suburbs, where are all the red flags and the hurrahs? Nowhere. Nothing but God's wind sweeping across the world, the suburbs of the world, beyond Belyaevo to the ring-road outside Moscow, and beyond it to the patient Volgograd lands, a sad, half-empty place – the milk is burning in her breast, just a copse, a field, trains to Volgograd, my wretched native land, Lord embrace me with your earth and your smooth, smooth snow.

It's quiet and bright up here, all the windows are looking at me, I've just come out of the bath, strawberry soap, head spinning, I lost Alyosha with his cupid mouth – someone's ringing at the door. Who is it? I don't want to go, I want to stay here staring at the lights through the window. They're ringing again, they know I'm in because they can see the strip of light under my door, someone's standing out there ringing my bell.

Hi there, Anna Ivanovna! Didn't you know it was me?

No, I didn't know, didn't see, didn't call, didn't lift my eyes – there's a programme on the box, Alyosha – the box I said, not the bottle, it's that spy programme called *Seventeen Moments of Spring*. He's still at his granny's, he's only little, moments of spring, yes I'm fine, there's nothing wrong with me, help I'm going to faint, right here at your feet. What do you mean hiding? The flat's mine. What have I to hide? Why would I hide, Alyosha? Far beyond Moscow are the flickering lights of the Volgograd lands,

Alyosha's there on his sledge. No don't put on *It's No Good, My Friend*, I'm knackered from work, let's play my record of love songs and listen to the storm. *The finest, proudest ma-an in the world...* Mum, please take my Alyosha, you can see I've a fever. Go with Granny, Alyosha, here's your dummy. It's winter again, and Dyrdybaev's back, a good, kind, thoughtful man with big hands. Your eyes are black, your mouth is hot – why are you grinning, don't you like a Russian breast full of milk? Go down on your knees!

You're a good woman I'm telling you, a good, kind woman, I'll trample on you in silence and go. Remember me? I'm Dyrdybaev, I've come to set you on fire! Hey, she's on fire already! You're a good, good woman, that's why I keep on coming back.

Oh, Dyrdybaev!

You're honest, you're fair, you're for people, you're against war, you're good.

Dyrdybaev!

I'm leaving you again. My black eyes torment you.

Lord, look at the storm outside – I'm for people, I'm against war, I want peace, the storm's secret tenderness for my fever. Mum, give me back my Alyosha to cool us...

Hello good woman, it's me again, Dyrdybaev. I had a job tracking you down. I'll never forget you. I always remember good people, I carry them forever in my heart.

Dyrdybaev, please get me a ticket for Volgograd, my son's burning, he caught a chill on his sledge, his granny wasn't watching him, he's too small, I have to go, do you understand me?

I understand you, good woman, you're so clean, a proper housewife, I love you. I bought my wife Anna Ivanovna a wall unit, I'd do anything for my family, I used to be full of doubts, I love my wife, I respect her as a woman, a mother, a singer – she's leader of a boys' choir, she steps forward and sings with a tight little voice, and the choir follows her into the fire. I'm a chauffeur, I take all my money home, I bought her a wall unit and a three-piece suite, but I never forget a good person like you.

Listen, my friend. Mother called me just before you came, she says Alyosha's feverish and needs milk. Yes, touch me here, yes it's burning there, I must hurry to Volgograd, to my storm-white far-off boy...

You're a good woman, lie down.

Like this?

Undress yourself for me, storm-white woman, and I'll cover you with my shadow.

Was I okay?

Alyosha, my Alyosha, my fever in the storm, I'm on fire, I'm blocked by the window and I can't get milk to you, it's splashing in the wind. Someone dropped us from their weak arms into the seething storm. There's a leaf flashing past! Funny to think of gardens in this snow...

Oh it's you again, Anna Ivanovna, you must go, no you tell me to go. No, your Dyrdybaev didn't come. You want me to fall at your feet sobbing, biting, dying? Your black man wasn't here! How can I tell you about those black nights and Tartar eyes? He never came near me, you're a good kind woman, can't you see I'm dying, bitter, numb? Isn't Alyosha big yet?

Gardens explode in the storm, splashing, whirling past, white enemies seethe and snarl. *Dear Dyrdybaev, I've decided to write to you. I rushed away from that stormy night and now you have a son called Alyosha, white and fluffy, funny as the storm, but flooded with your Tartar darkness. Your Anna.*

Hot brow on the pane, freezing fever, my sick child in a distant town alone with his grandma, I must go to him. That's him flying through the storm, I saw him!

Alyosha's mum goes crazy. If she had wisely clutched her hot fluffy head and stared through the window, rocking with pain, she would have seen it lying out there in the storm. Instead of shaking and groaning, she should have looked coolly at herself. But it's no use, she can't wait, the fever burns her head with its blue and gold.

When they run in to help her they find her lying on the floor, and when they push open the window for air, a parrot flies in. It's not frozen in the storm, it's flashing there green and patient, waiting to be let in. He from his great height can wait – mother in her peace and warmth cannot. She is taken to hospital, and the parrot is given corn and a mirror for love. She, Mum, conscientiously forgets everything in hospital, then finally comes to and is happy. Alyosha is brought to her, the parrot flies in from the storm to live with them forever, and everything sorts itself out.

Most boys are fascinated by basements and roofs, but with Alyosha it's a dim, mysterious janitor called Dyrdybaev. Dyrdybaev has a gnarled hand full of keys, and he unlocks the inaccessible.

"Don't touch, it'll kill you," he says. Dancing after him like the wind, Alyosha stands on tiptoe behind Dyrdybaev's bent back and looks into the "don't touch". Wires twist, fizzle and flash. Dyrdybaev pokes at them, sighs, stamps his feet, then locks it all up again with his key.

Alyosha takes wing and flies off to the bushes to study the gnarled one with watchful golden eyes. He looks at the world, he listens to the light and the blood in his body, he doesn't know why he must tease the yellow Tartar. He goes to the playground and spreads his limbs on the iron training bars. Dyrdybaev wheezes and bends over his broom. Alyosha lies on the bars dreaming with his cat's eye. Dyrdybaev scrapes the ground. Alyosha swings a sandal from his toe. Dyrdybaev sweeps up cigarette-ends and scraps of paper. Alyosha goes on swinging his sandal. Dyrdybaev smooths the grass with his broom. Alyosha drops his sandal into the silence. Dyrdybaev drops his broom with a roar and chases after him, but cool happy Alyosha is wriggling away and teasing him from behind a poplar tree, shouting: "Hey mister, give me back my shoe!"

Leaves splash, laughter splashes in the boy's golden face as the Tartar raises his strong arms to the tree and the sky:

"Oh Allah, give me that boy, I'll kick his heart in!" His dark, un-Russian face turns green: "I'll tell your mum, d'you hear!" The boy is silent. As he examines the Tartar's crooked smoky face he forgets to laugh, he becomes bright and sad. The Tartar grows lithe and cheerful, his face shines with stars, the shade of the leaves, the green shadow of summer light on the dark face raised to your foot.

"Stop teasing the Tartar, Alyosha, don't be naughty. Eat up, here's a clean shirt, the girls never stop phoning."

"I hate soup, I don't want it!"

"Make yourself something then, whatever you like."

"Granny gave me cakes, nice things – you can't cook!"

"Here, take this and buy some cakes."

She goes to her room to be sad. It makes Alyosha smile. Narrowing his golden eyes, he looks at the wall and sees his mother sitting there with her golden eyes, arranging the pencils on her table, moving a vase – a mum who'll get up, go to the window and lie spread out on the pane. Alyosha narrows his eyes and grins. The bird jumps on to his shoulder, and pecks his cheek. Alyosha absent-mindedly kisses the bird and goes out to join a fencing club.

"Look Mum, I came top!" he says. "See my certificate!"

"Clever boy!" says Mum, kissing his forehead. She keeps her lips pressed to his forehead. "Have you a fever? Show me your throat."

He pokes out his tongue.

She sadly shakes her head. He narrows his eyes and stares at her face, then looks down and grins. "Sorry Mum, I won't do it again."

"When I grow up I'll be in charge and I'll buy her everything," he thinks. "We'll look in the mirror together, as if by accident – we'll pretend we're going to the window to get something, and she'll say: 'Let me show you something on the window-sill, you won't believe it.' And I'll say: 'Okay!' We pass the mirror, look up and freeze, staring into it, going into it, turning into two little boys."

My storm boy, my cloud boy, my unbaptised breast.

Mum potters about the flat, passing years grow dim.

There's a cripple on television. Alyosha laughs. Mum frowns at him and switches it off. Young men come to see Alyosha. He shouts at them and gives orders, or orders his Mum: "If they call, tell 'em I'm dead!"

From time to time Mum absent-mindedly observes: "What a wicked heart you have, Alyosha!" Alyosha looks down at his shoulder and the bird gives him a peck. But it turns out the little green bird has a wicked heart too, it rushes at people's faces, flaps around the room and won't let anyone near Alyosha, hopping on his shoulder, swearing, screeching, stamping, pecking his cheek and biting his lips till they bleed.

Mum brushes the bird off, and it angrily flaps away. "The plumber came today but the tap's still leaking, and he stole my nail-scissors," she grumbles. Alyosha is irritated with his Mum's pointed pink finger-nails. "Serves you right, sitting at the window doing your nails with the wind sloping outside the window," he thinks, but he doesn't say so, for he is a loving, respectful son. Instead he says: "Tell the Housing Office." Mum is alarmed. "Don't you dare, he'll get into trouble!" Alyosha grins at this mother of his. He runs whooping down the street with the other boys making mischief, the spirit of the suburbs, broken glass in the grass, trees, a wasteland, the patient sky. They set fire to the letter-boxes of the poor, ugly, faded people, they stare at the good-looking ones in sad silence, and they don't fall in love with anyone.

Mum brushes the bird off, and it angrily flaps away.

At six in the morning in cheerless Belyaevo, people come out into the bitter air, baring their teeth at the frozen ground and accidentally warming each other on the buses. Mum's soul is bright as she makes lemonade, kisses the bird and stares in bewilderment out of the window, where people stand patiently baring their teeth at the cold expanse, and the air howls from the sky to the ground.

Mum and Alyosha catch snatches of songs and quiet music from the radio. *Winter Blows the Snow into My Face*, and in the evening after work, *I Shout to the Wind*. People pour from the bus, the office, the factory.

"We still have cheese and sausage left. Hurry while stocks last!"

Groaning, Mum drops her face in her hands. "Why do they tell us lies, Alyosha? I don't understand! The lift's broken, but they run panting up seventeen flights of stairs to tell us lies about sausages!"

Alyosha looks down to his shoulder and kisses the bird.

"And who are those foreign pilots hanging about in our hallway? Why have they come?"

Alyosha kisses the bird, and the bird kisses Alyosha's lips till they bleed.

"And who sent us those bunches of jasmine? Look how angrily they've been snapped off. They scare me!"

Alyosha throws the jasmine out of the window. He laughs, and the nameless pilots look at the spiteful boy laughing as the jasmine circles slowly downwards.

Narrow your two mortal trembling eyes, my empty-seething garden. First comes winter, then summer. Winter is sweeter than summer, more bitter than boredom, the sweet boredom of my empty-seething youth. Grieving like the evening twilight, Mum clutches her hot head and drags herself down seventeen flights of stairs, her mouth weeping. She stops by the landing windows, thinking about life, the storm, that summer when Mum and me looked out of the window and the storm howled and we sighed with excitement, squeezing each others' fingers and drinking it all in. The storm swept across the broad green clump of trees, the copse, the shrubs on the pavements, the thickets of the common, on to the gentle fields, and sweetly over the edge of the world. The green trembled at the hungriness of the meeting, then all of a sudden it stopped. We were scared that this was the end, but then the sun swam out, the green summer sparkled forth with the blush of winter and everyone in Belyaevo sighed – this was the proof! An extraordinary life.

Mum stands at the landing windows, yellow as the

vanishing spots of light in the windows opposite, blue as the distant shadows on the pale earth of winter, and she remembers the marvellous day that summer and wants it back again. The wind howls over the earth and piles up the snow at the bus-stops. At the edge of the world a factory puffs smoke. Mum waits patiently for the cold, not seeing, not understanding. She freezes by the draughty windows, then she remembers her destination and goes on down. The people she passes all take the lift. "You'll catch your death!" they say. She grins, looks away and says: "Forgive me!" It's not clear if they do. She goes down, down, down to the very ground and a bit beneath it, where the Maintenance Room is. I can't see, I don't know, I don't remember, I didn't look, I froze, I ran away! In the Maintenance Room, filled with chairs, brooms and Mayday declarations, sits a small quiet man diligently cutting school leaflets into tiny petals. He turns them into faded flowers and glues them to stiff twigs, singing a lively song from some distant village as he works. Masses of dead-flowering bushes stand in the corner waiting for the Mayday parade. A naked bulb shines above his head. As this honest, hard-working life ticks on in the basement Mum throws open the door, stands right there in the doorway like a drunken person, and stretches out her weak arms in grief and guilt, then breaks the circle with the sounds of running away.

"Dyrdybaev, forgive me!" she calls.

"No!"

Sleep now, sleep Alyosha, swaying as you breathe. Remember when I was young? When I was five?

I am five years old, sitting in the noisy blue smoke of a bar, wearing my big white rabbit-fur coat. I'm thinking: "If she acts up I'll smack her, but if she finishes her milk I'll kiss her and praise her to the skies! But what if she runs away? What's she staring at? What if she's upset? Let her act up, I'll not touch her! Why should I? I love her!" So they humiliate me instead. "Bloody kid, finish it up!" But I

don't want it now – later! I want my eyes to keep looking,
I want my dad and the other blokes to forget me, shrieking
and snarling around me like they're sick, grabbing their
cold beer and blowing on it, yelling: "Get your guns, boys!
Oil your rifles! The animal got your mum, shut up and
drink your milk! She's just a kid but she's spoilt rotten.
Look, the animal's prowling outside in the snow!"

My dad promised me a kitten, so there! My dad doesn't
tell lies, I'm going to have a kitten for a friend! I keep
waiting for my little orange tabby friend, the girl and her
fairy kitten living in a magic house! Then suddenly it
dawns on me, I stand right-up though I'm way too short,
and I see him come in (my eyes have been looking around
all this time, remember), and I see this weird person come
in and I gasp. He's dead drunk, funny, probably young.
My eyes like two hunting dogs can see he doesn't understand anything, nor why he's come. Why am I a drunken
idiot? he asks, as the barmaid hands him a mug. She yells
at him, he doesn't understand, he shakes his head and
laughs, she waves her arm, who cares, he's drunk! He
stands there in front of everyone, looks around and drinks
up his beer in front of them like an idiot, and they shove
him and shout at him like an idiot, but he laughs at them.
His hand sails up with the beer, his Adam's apple bobs, he
drinks and looks around like an idiot to see where to put
his empty glass. Just then Dad and the other blokes
remember me, shouting at me and pushing my nose in the
milk. It splashes my face and blinds me and I nearly drown
in it, but I drink it up, anything so Dad will keep his
promise and I'll get my little tabby freckled kitten. When
they let me go, towering over me and shouting about guns
and bolts, I see him standing there beside me looking at
me. He wonders if I'll smile at him or not, and I look at
him not knowing if his lips will tremble or give a sad smile
at the little milk-splashed girl. I have a rash on my hands,
they hurt till they bleed, you couldn't bear it! My coat's
extra big so I can grow into it and it'll last me a long
time, and I'm so small inside I'm buried in it, so you grab

the sleeves thinking they're my arms, and my felt boots keep falling off. I blow at your gold and cry at your fierceness. "I want my kitten now, you pig!" And he sees me, he sees me for ever, Christmas, namedays and birthdays, and curling his lip to show his gleaming ruthless teeth he goes off, stone-cold sober, for ever, to the edge.

Dad finds out I've wet myself and I'm sitting in cold trousers, and he shouts at me for being a naughty, stupid little girl who can't even ask to go, chattering away and enjoying herself with the hunters and lumberjacks – they spoil the kid to death, giving her sweets and showing her their hunting dogs, big as horses, and she whispers in their furry ears as they stupidly wag their tails at her. In two years she'll be at school and she'll have forgotten about everything, she'll dream her dreams and she won't have to drink her milk, she's a bad girl, that's all, and her kitten's dead! Don't yell, stop howling, it's bedtime, she's only little, she's sobbed her heart out and fallen asleep, stop shouting boys, the kid's asleep, hat tipped over one ear, carry her to bed, we'll shoot the animal tomorrow.

Dyrdybaev goes through life thinking y.

The District Office asks her straight out what she's up to. "We've had enough of you and your golden face, tell us the truth. Men dropping like flies around you, Aeroflot pilots, jasmine flowers torn off for nothing – the whole of Belyaevo knows about you. You can't mean it!"

"I do!" she sobs.

"That spring," she says, "the sad spring of the suburbs, I look out of the window and see flower-beds all around the yard, everything green. It's so hot Dyrdybaev's stripped off to the waist, the back and shoulders of a young man. He's tending our trees, he looks so sweet and funny I leave the window and forget him. It only hurts in the evening."

That spring she coos to Dyrdybaev: "Shall I paint your apple trees for you?"

"No!" he says, his face like thunder. His words lash her heart.

"I want a snow-storm," she says. "I want jasmine, a storm of jasmine, you flying with the wings of an eagle, me peering from the garden of sweet coldness – look at Dyrdybaev up there! Young men drop dead but I don't care, Dyrdybaev's flying in the sky, and if we become small we're just seeds from the berries! You give me a dead bird, I give you a splinter of bright mirror. No one will ask what the children are playing, the grown-ups will go to the District Office once and for all." That's what she says to him all in a rush that spring.

Dyrdybaev lives in the world and thinks *y*. People's words are too small for him, he shudders at their word-poverty. He doesn't speak, he loves to clean the earth, to smooth the snow, comb the grass, paint the apple-trees. He doesn't love it, he doesn't know who he is. When he sees his face in the mirror he scowls at the black foreigner before him, and the Tartar scowls back. He turns to go out, and carries in his heart all day the troubling memory of the Tartar in the mirror. By evening he has forgotten about it. Does he spend the day moping about the Tartar in the mirror, and wish him dead for being so fierce and foreign? No, such feelings are too small for Dyrdybaev, like people's words. Y, the great *y*, is the only thing in his heart. There's Storm Woman. Storm Woman makes him angry. He sees her and thinks *y*, and anger flashes to the sky. Dyrdybaev meets Storm Woman like he meets the Tartar in the mirror. He looks down and goes out, his back hunched, dragging his spade over the ground with a grating sound. He knows that Storm Woman from her high window can see him touching the apple-trees below, as she looks down from the sky to the earth and to earthy Dyrdybaev. For years she looks down as Dyrdybaev walks over the earth with bent back, pruning the trees in her yard. The crown of her head reaches to the blue above, trees spring from her gaze and reach out to her.

One poplar grows tall, and from this tree Dyrdybaev is teased by a golden boy, a monster, like *y*, great *y*, muddling all his thoughts and the world. "I'm Dyrdybaev,

and Storm Woman makes me angry." Dyrdybaev wants a
peacock tail reaching to the sky. Quietly fanning his tail,
he looks at Storm Woman with the eyes of its feathers. She
moans, he falls to the ground, and y flashes to the heavens.

Oh Allah, throw over the city a tight-meshed hammock
of seething jasmine – people will think it's a snow-storm
but it's your net over the town! Abandon me to your stuffy
sky hammock, Allah, rock it over the city and suburbs so
people will think Moscow is blinded by the storm. Look,
there's Dyrdybaev out there again with his wooden spade,
scratching the snow, piling the sweet coldness into drifts.
He doesn't know he's District Office janitor Dyrdybaev.

Snow descends on the wastes of Belyaevo, calm and
beautiful on every side, as far as the factory. The snow
makes the night bright, everyone is sleeping, the air around
the tall houses is quiet. Dyrdybaev walks along scratching
quietly with his special light wooden spade, throwing the
snow from side to side as the District Office told him to.
The gleaming snow laughs and sparkles as it falls from his
spade, Belyaevo laughs and sparkles on every side.

Suddenly he stands rooted to the spot. Staring at his
spade, he realises he doesn't need it and tosses it softly on
the snow. The snow sighs as far as the factory, and
Dyrdybaev strides quietly ahead, his back bent with horror
at the whiteness and limitlessness. Then suddenly it comes
to him. Trembling with hope, he steps forward and draws
a circle in the snow around her funny cold feet, so his
Storm Woman in furs can stand in splendour in the middle
of the circle, proud of herself, admiring herself, while
Dyrdybaev lies beside her not letting anyone in, and the
limitless whiteness draws back. Then an even stronger
thought comes to him, and he enters the circle with her, as
though entering the mirror, reaching the stranger at last
and meeting him. Understanding everything, she steps back,
no longer hungry, and shows the shaken Dyrdybaev two
little blue footprints, into each of which he carefully fits
his own foot.

She says: "All right Dyrdybaev, I, Storm Woman

Ivanovna, will talk to you like this!". And the cold, funny woman jumps out of the circle with the wooden spade on her storm-white shoulder and goes off to the edge.

Then a piece of the mesh in Allah's hammock breaks, and through it flies a man, black with fear, his mouth twisted in a wordless shriek. Cutting the air from sky to earth, he lands on the two blue footprints in the circle, and Dyrdybaev falls in a handful of muscles, brown eyes and bones. No wings. Allah's abandoned jasmine hammock sways, glimpses of his blue sky flash through the broken mesh, and Moscow thinks, what a storm!

That winter, I unthinkingly went to a group of young strangers to mock love in the wind.

The sleeping boy lies trustingly sprawled out, a rash of birthmarks like mocking stars on his chest, covered in smooth hair like a dark bird, his pink breath, the shadow of his eyelashes. Irresistible. Cursed and cast out, I know now that I must roam and struggle. Black bastard, you have cast your shadow over me!

I creep to your door, black Dyrdybaev, and go through to where you scratch, wheeze and piteously call my name. We nod. You ask me to take you to the sleeping young man so trustingly sprawled out. I say to you: "Let's open up his chest and see what's inside." You nod, your dark face shining. We hesitate a moment, afraid to touch him, then together we hurl ourselves at him, sink our nails deep in his chest and prize open his crunching ribs. His dying mouth gives a soft moan of surprise as we move apart his hot breastbones. Inside there's nothing. Just milk. To the very edge. We were wrong. He's just his mother's boy.

Howling with sadness and rage, sticky with the milk from the dead man's chest, we roll about in spasms of fury and despair, glued together, monster devouring monster, two smoky-green creatures with gold blue intelligent eyes.

The South

There, at dawn, rush in the waves
To the sandy, empty shore.
Pushkin

The little person was washed up to my feet, pale, smoky
eyes on a small dark face. He was pulled back, belly down
on the shingle. He laughed, to make me happy, and picked
up pebbles. The waves washed him in again. I was cold
from the water and high up, and he was charming me. Far
off behind him, behind everyone, the sky laid its trusting
breast on the gentle sea. Don't trust the sea, little man, the
sea can be wild.

Then an entreaty flashed in his gentle eyes; realising
that I knew more than I should, he begged forgiveness, a
little boy poking gently at my poor feet.

Oh, to forget for a thousand years that the world
exists, then dimly glimpse its existence, suffer in agony and
be sad for it, and wake with the sea reaching the sky and
someone's little son splashing at one's feet.

Crowds of people came south. They saved up their
money, went down the mines, worked flat-out. Rough,
hardworking people, they sat from dawn to dusk on the
beach wanting their money's worth of southern sun.
Crowds of people came south to enjoy themselves

and live, Ukrainian people. Roast chicken and honey drinks were sold everywhere – they ate all they wanted.

Olya kept looking behind her at the beach people, and moved away from the boy in the water. Georgian words deafened and frightened her. "Everything's foreign here," she thought, "there's the sea, but I'm not alone. You can't drink it in with your eyes, so I'll leave still thirsty."

Weary of the beach she walked into town, to the Waterfall café, where she ordered a raw egg yolk with sugar and sat down. Moving aside the plates of chicken bones, she put down her glass and sat in the heat and dirt listening to the foreign music. The music was frightening.

Something had happened to her over the past year; she had sickened inside. There were no particular symptoms, the blood just seemed to tire of going around her body, and she was still so young. She started taking vitamins and eating properly, but the invisible power of life kept ebbing away. She grew melancholy, her head drooped, her supply of friends dried up and she was alone. Sometimes it's good to be alone, to cure oneself of people. But as the fleshless power of life drained from her body and she grew thinner, she decided to go south and shake it off, to remember in the sun and the water why it is necessary to live and how to nourish her body; to languish in the sea, unable to utter its name as it washed pure her soul and her nerves, to wonder at the profusion of southern roses, and listen to the hot, bitter southern language hopelessly clamouring for more than can be found.

Yet once there, she could see she wasn't part of the general happiness. She ate badly, she could not swim far. Not for her the pure sea; for her, the human sea of unknown bodies washing each other away. Even this might have healed her sadness, but the warmth of life did not return and the darkness inside her grew still stronger.

"I've so many more years left, is there nothing for me?" she wondered. "I need something strong. Like all those years ago, when I was a child..."

There was Tanya, yes Tanya, from the flat below.

Tanya was a thief, but playing with her was always interesting and full of surprises. They once dipped their tongues in a glass of vodka left over from a funeral. They sneaked up to the attic to look down on their yard from a new angle. One day Olya stole something; she didn't enjoy it, and the tears welled up and she felt scared. She often went off Tanya to read books and dream of journeys and a dog.

Once the boy from upstairs was coming down to play in the yard, and Tanya said: "Let's beat up the German!"

"Why? What kind of German is he?" Olya asked. "He doesn't even go to school yet!"

The German was wearing a clean, freshly-ironed shirt.

"They killed our people!" whispered Tanya so the German wouldn't hear, his bare legs reverently mastering each step in turn.

"You don't understand," Tanya jabbed Olya with her elbow, "your mum's nice, she sings at the factory club, you don't know fascists."

The German came closer, ready for summer in the yard. He could still remember his room, with Mother and soup with meatballs, but now he had to let Mother and the room go, because his whole body was poised to leap into the grass, the noise of sparrows, flies, mosquitoes and July squabbles in the yard.

"We must smash the Germans for the Reds!" said Tanya. "Are you a Pioneer or not?"

The German was bathed in the light from the dingy landing window, downy hair flashed on his legs. Olya remembered bloody films about wild beasts and fascist predators, and everything trembled and got mixed up inside her. Here he stood, the German on our steps, swathed in a cloud of fascism. They grabbed the German. He had never noticed us until we grabbed him; he looked at us in surprise and with difficulty, caught by two girl Pioneers between Mother and summer. All the important things happen in summer.

"Say you're a fascist," said Tanya. "Then we'll kick you and let you go!"

"Then you can go," added Olya.

"Or else you can cry," said Tanya.

"I'm not a fascist!" said the prisoner. "Filthy scum!"

"So little, and already swearing," noted Olya, surprised.

"Say you're a German!" said Tanya.

"A fascist!" added Olya.

"I'm not a fascist, I'm a Red officer!" he declared, preparing to die, whereupon a button flew off his shirt. They had to let him go then, flushed from his torments and hardened in their hands. They knew no tortures apart from kicking and slapping, and they didn't even know for sure that he was a fascist.

He ran off down to the yard, carrying his tears with him. "See how he didn't cry," said Tanya. "He must be a fascist!"

Nothing happened to the girls – the fascist obviously said nothing to his fascist mother – but Olya went off Tanya after that and didn't see her again. Tanya's brother came out of prison, a grown-up, red-faced boy smoking sulkily by the door. There were secrets, you weren't supposed to say hello to them. The children were sullen and beautiful, they had a secret, and she didn't want to see them again...

Washed away by the wind, the sea's sparkle shines on from its own reserves, rising from a tiny ray of light and glimmering there, then flooded by tiny suns which stretch like a mica membrane to the next cloud. There is a man on the jetty. Smaller than everyone else except the children, he is closer to the sea – even, curiously, to the sky. Every day his enflamed gaze angrily scans the shoreline to the sky. It is as though he has fallen on to his knees from fear of life, and is unable to stand up again. Since he cannot live with people in this condition, he takes on the waves instead, with the resolute heaving of his chest. The sea needs no legs and cannot go away, but a person, even without legs, can push himself on to the jetty every day in his wooden frame and breathe his hot, rasping breath over the sea. The sea is like flight. The man is smaller than everyone but the children, and his eyes break against people's legs, the dirty asphalt, the stains and pebbles on the jetty. The children grow bigger, and games are spread out for them in the world below, but there is nothing there for this heavy full-grown half-man, so he drags himself off to look at the sea until it tweaks his eyes and he sees it is lighter than the sky – yes, you could fly in it!

Weak and empty with sadness, Olya had decided to heal herself. She was given the number of an expensive doctor, Alla Sergeevna, who specialised in nerves and general vitality, and ordered her compellingly to come over. Olya liked her at once, cheerfully surrounded by beautiful things, expensive-smelling and evenly tanned under a sun-lamp, with roses and a little dog, and the happy brown shine of the expensive doctor's made-up eyes. They ate sweets and, whenever the phone rang, Alla Sergeevna would get angry, to show Olya how much more interesting she was than any of the calls. Olya liked this trick. She also liked not having to discuss her ailments, trained as she was from childhood not to talk about big things, as though when you do some strength goes out of your heart forever. Alla Sergeevna evidently took her responsibilities seriously, observing Olya and her words, leading her through the dark history of a burglary in her flat and watching to see if Olya was following. Wasn't her head powerfully weak, burdened by thoughts of life, wondering if it could still live and think like everyone else? If this was the case, it would be possible to cure Olya and restore her to happiness.

"They took everything – rings, brooches, bracelets, two Japanese rugs, a pure gold watch with diamond chips, fur coats, some linings.... We had literally nothing but the clothes we stood up in! Three years have passed, and we're still feeling the effects."

"They must have known you had it."

"I managed to save just one ring, which I wore to go out. Everything else they took. I love beautiful things, anyone can see that. The police said: 'Take whatever you want, it'll go anyway.' They had everything – vases, record-players. But we didn't want someone else's stuff. Nothing of ours was found. A long list of valuables, but we could see they weren't even looking for them!"

"The police couldn't have taken it. Unless you saw some funny policeman."

"You're right there! They were charged, and the police chief and the prosecutor both went to prison. In each of their flats they found fifty kilograms of gold!"

"So it was obviously them, Alla Sergeevna."

Alla Sergeevna treated Olya expensively and cheerfully, writing dozens of prescriptions for herbs and infusions, selling her face lotion and a sun-lamp, and whipping up a special skin cream from rare Indian herbs.

"I shall give myself back my zest for life. Look at everything here – it's so precious! The little dog with his delicate body and soft, soft fur, washed with sweet-smelling shampoo," Olya thought. "I shall go down, down into the spiral of material connections, I shall get close to these people, I shall have a telephone, servants, the fine petals of foreign clothes, a dog like this on my knees, a deep sofa. I am beautiful, I shall have rich husbands, I shall marry an Italian, I shall take my dog to Italy..."

The thing was, Olya was already married. She was very fond of her husband, the dark and gentle Alik, who adored her and was forever touching her, and was always so tender. They lived in the country, far away from everyone. In winter, when the dacha was cut off by the snow, Alik would sit quietly by the open stove, the snow falling quietly outside the window, the gate banging in the wind.

"No visitors," thought Olya. "This is life. Here is warmth and love. Out there is the snow, the passing trains, the wind, and something sad is roaming in the pine trees. The houses here have no people, only ours is filled with talk and the smell of food. You can live here until youth leaves the body and there's no money, no place in the society of people, and it's time to look for new support."

"We'll be together forever," Alik said hurriedly to her.

"How do you know what life will be like?" she asked.

"What are you saying?" he said, frightened.

"We change a thousand times," she was fond of saying.

"I know who I am," he said.

Yet he was the first to change. She saw him grow fearful and trembling, as if through the stillness of their world he could hear other voices, for in their silent life every rustle and squeak rang out so clearly. He started hiding from her and weeping. "Let him go back to his mother," Olya thought. He avoided her eyes and hunched dejectedly over his tea. The heat of the stove still kept them warm in the country storm, the cat was with them, and they had enough to eat, but Alik had a dream.

He dreamed he was in a glass hall, with an entrance like a hotel lobby and smooth, dark doors. It was an exhibition, but more sumptuous than an exhibition. Standing on black pedestals in the brightness of the hall were animals made from expensive coloured glass. The beauty of these creations pierced Alik's heart. Looking more closely, he saw an animal furtively stir as it changed its weary pose, and he realised the creations were alive – cats, rabbits, bears, foxes, crawling creatures, scorpions and lions, miracles in glass, all breathing and pulsating. Shaken by his emotions, Alik wandered on enchanted through the hall, widening into the distance, and saw that no two animals were alike in species, fur-colour or glassy luminescence. Alik was bewitched. He could still look to the right, where the window was dark but there was a sense of real life, warm people. Yet he didn't look, and the window shrank back. The animals settled down, snarling, gurgling and whistling. No longer concealing their movements, they brazenly exposed their glassy smoothness, lending an unimaginable, trembling suppleness to the glass.

Everything in Alik sang and responded. "Yes, this is how it is!" whispered the young man's pale lips. The animals did not jump from their pedestals as he passed, but gazed at him and followed him with their muzzles, bared teeth gleaming, pawing the air and howling invitingly. He already sensed that this was some awful, fateful trap. But then the hall started tipping downwards into a bright, blue half-light, and Alik unhurriedly slipped down, down into an oval room, where a young black cat – a panther, prince of the realm – reclined in state on a gleaming green pedestal. The panther stood up on its beautiful legs and a groan of ecstasy went around, so beautiful was this black prince of the feline species, so powerful yet so small, cleverly fitting into the space of one's hand. Alik bowed twice and was brought to the prince. Do not leave, beautiful panther, stretch and gleam on your emerald pedestal, open wide your little red mouth, my black lord, demand your sacrifices, for you are better than anyone!

The dream was broken by applause, and Alik awoke forever different.

Olya saw him once in town. He was strikingly conspicuous amongst the other pedestrians. Olya nearly wept: a whitish skull-cap on top of dirty, unkempt hair twisted into tight curls, sunken cheeks covered in stubble, shuffling along like an old man with bent back and two dark eyes staring fixedly through the life around them.

The southern night is dark, dense and damp. At night the earth of the South is visibly alive. Olya rented a hut at the top of the hill, where the solitary bus would wind its way up past six stops. The landlady had many people staying there, but as Olya got up late and came back late she didn't know them all by sight. In the yard stood a table swollen from the night rain, and at night the lamp above it would be lit and the holiday-makers would play cards. In the evening after cards Olya, in her hut, would listen to them talking.

Combing the wet, lifeless hair of her youngest daughter, a sullen almost speechless child, a woman from the mining town of Makeevka would tell stories to the deliciously frightened children in a special distant, unhurried voice:

"On the edge of town was a brick factory. The bricks were baked in special ovens, like ours, only massive. There was this old night watchman. One night he couldn't sleep because he knew something was up, so he went over to the ovens and saw that one of them hadn't been put out and was blazing away. Then he heard someone screaming and sobbing, and he saw two men dragging along a young girl. She was all tied up and couldn't defend herself, but she was a real beauty, with big blue eyes and long snowy-blond hair. One of the men grabbed a poker and opened the oven, and flames gushed out. As they pushed the girl towards the oven they didn't see her purposely dropping her bag a little way away, but the watchman noticed where it fell. As the men yelled and cursed and beat the weeping girl, pushing her closer and closer to the blaze, she lost the strength to resist. Then the watchman saw how young she was, and he felt so sorry for her he left his hiding place, and the girl saw him too, and they looked at each other. The men struggled with the girl, pushing her into the flames. The girl's eyes met those of the watchman and he saw the terror in her eyes, then she signalled with her head to where her bag lay. He nodded that he understood, then the men pushed the girl into the oven. The watchman forgot to hide and closed his eyes so he wouldn't have to see the girl burn. He heard the oven-door crash as the men slammed it after her. For a moment the fire was silent, then terrible moans came from the flames. The blaze roared, and the men bolted from the crime, not noticing the old man. When he saw they were gone he grabbed the bag of documents and ran to open the oven-door, but all that remained of the girl was a brooch. Weeping, he took the hot brooch to the police, who were able to track down the criminals, and the watchman identified them immediately. It turned out the girl had beaten the men at cards. They hadn't wanted to kill her because she was so beautiful and they all loved her, but that was their law, and their leader said they had to go through with it. The men admitted everything and named all the members of the gang, and on that night their hair turned white..."

The southern night, foreign and luxurious, roamed

blindly through the foliage. Olya could hardly breathe in her damp sheets. The children outside the window were thoughtful, pitying the dead girl and happy that the villains were punished.

The woman from Makeevka waited all year to bring her daughter to the sea. In Makeevka, people can't breathe, their lungs are choked with coal. The woman was sunburnt and wary, cleaning her lungs in the sea air and not believing her daughter would ever leave Makeevka. Once Olya went up to the girl and asked her name. The child looked angrily at her and ran away.

"Come here to Mummy, Gala!" called the woman.

The little girl hid herself behind her mother.

"What class are you in at school?" Olya asked dutifully.

"Year three," said the woman grudgingly, shielding Gala with her arm.

"Don't tell her, Mum."

"You've a frightened daughter!" Olya laughed.

"Come on Gala, let's go," the woman led her daughter away, leaving Olya alone on the bench. A large-headed night moth crawled over the rain-swollen table. Someone had left a bathing-cap there. Gala crept back to retrieve it. Olya covered her eyes, pretending not to see. Gala hesitated, then thought of her thin hair sticking wetly to her scalp, and snatched the cap.

"Whoops Gala, don't fall!"

"Let me go!" Gala sunk her teeth into Olya's white arm. Olya opened her arms in surprise, and Gala ran off, cat-like, with her cap. What sort of town was Makeevka?

Kostya, the landlady's son, wandered into the yard holding a toy motor-car. Kostya loved sweets and cars, he even had a model railway, every boy's dream. Olya made him paper aeroplanes which flew like butterflies, and Kostya was delighted. Once she made him a paper frog. "Look at its big mouth! Quack, quack! It's funny!" she said. But Kostya didn't understand. Olya was bothered by the boy, his dreamy soul disturbed her, he made her want to fall asleep in the hay dreaming of the harvest and the smell of the country. But they didn't have that kind of country in the South, everything was different here.

Kostya had a bowl full of black cherries. One of the cherries had burst, staining the water in the bowl pink. Kostya watched everything closely. He knew they knew about his sleepy soul, but somewhere in his childish indolence a hot coal smouldered, which sometimes burned him and was reflected in his smoky eyes. While the other boys were larking around, Kostya went off with his toy cars, but when they sat down in the evening to play cards he often won. Kostya was fifteen. When the children met up again that summer they had all grown bigger, even Gala had stubbornly pushed up on her own through the winter. Kostya's mother fretted about how big the other children had grown. Andryusha was already doing his hair a special way and demanding clean shirts in the evening, while Kostya was still playing with his trains. When Kostya called him to look at them, Andryusha looked at Kostya, praised them guardedly and turned away. But of course he was a whole year older, Kostya's mother reminded herself. Andryusha leaned over the engine with his white shirt and neatly parted hair. "It's great, isn't it?" Kostya demanded excitedly, pointing to the little wheels and windows. How they had played together last year! "Yeah, it's great," agreed Andryusha, and went off with the big boys. The coal smouldered in Kostya's grey eyes.

"Winter is calmer for us," thought Kostya's mother. "The winds blow, people toboggan down the hill, the house howls and shakes in the storm, the torn-up sea gnaws at the town, the town breaks in the wind and wet, and at night the town is empty and the child is warm at home with his toys. Don't compare him with the others, there's no need. He's a sweet, quiet boy pushing his toy cars around the sofa, he doesn't hang out with the teenagers by the wild winter sea."

The toy train rushes round and round the room. "Next station!" shouts Kostya. "Play with me, Mum. I'm bored on my own in winter."

"Mummy has a headache."

"Will more boys come when it's summer? New ones?"

"Definitely!"

"Let's go! Next stop, Sochi!"

Olya invited Kostya to her room, to see how she lived.

"I know how you live, my mum makes your bed!" Kostya said.

Olya reached for his arm. He smiled and stretched out his limp hand to her.

"Let's go," she urged.

They went into her hut.

"Sit on the bed."

He sat down. The flame smouldered in his grey eyes.

"Do you like school?"

"Suppose so," he said.

"Do you have friends?"

"Suppose so." He tried to leave.

"Wait. We can play."

"Play what? There's nothing to play with."

"So what's this?" She handed the boy an embroidered, beaded make-up bag.

"It's beautiful," he said, admiring it.

"Open it!" she ordered, straightening her back so he wouldn't see her trembling.

He opened it. "There's make-up in here, all sorts of toys, everything a girl needs!"

"Smell it."

"Smells like flowers. Even stronger!"

"Do you like it?"

"Very much. Why do you wear no jewellery, just that plain ring?"

She twisted the ring on her finger.

"It won't come off."

"It's so plain, with no stone."

"I've always worn it, ever since I was a child. Don't look at it."

"Why do you wear it?"

"So I won't get lost, so people will know it's me – like

a bird. The bird flies off, but people know which bird it is because of the ring."

"Birds don't fly with rings on," said the boy.

"All right, let's play. Let's make ourselves beautiful, like princesses."

"But I'm a boy."

"It's only a game. Come on."

She opened a tube of lipstick, twisted the crimson cylinder out of its gold case, and put it carefully to the boy's mouth. His eyes darkened, he gulped. "What are you doing?"

"Close your mouth."

He closed his mouth.

"Relax your lips."

She rubbed the crimson over his mouth. The young face flared up impossibly.

Olya felt numb. "How beautiful, I want some too."

"Here, let me do it."

"You don't know how, you must do it with the lips."

"My lips?"

"Yes. But gently, so it won't smudge."

His eyes were veiled in smoke.

"We can't do that, we're different."

"What do you mean, different?"

"It's either two boys or two girls – with you it's not right."

"Don't be silly, I'm not a girl, I'm an old woman."

"You're not a woman, you're a girl."

"And you'll soon be a young man. Young men do it."

"Here, I'll do it gently."

"So it won't smudge."

"You must close your mouth, like I closed mine."

He bent his lips to her half-open mouth, then pulled away. She drew him to her neck, and they stayed like that for a while. Then she took away her hand. He looked warily at her and shrank back.

"See if you've done it evenly. Is it smudged?"

He watched her distrustfully.

"I bet you've smudged it. I did yours smoothly, but you've smudged mine!"

He glanced sullenly at her lips, then at her eyes.

"Are we playing or not?" Olya demanded angrily.

"I smudged it a bit," he admitted.

"Wipe it off then," she said, offended.

He stroked her lips with his fingers. His mouth was half-open with exertion, swollen from the kiss and smeared with traces of lipstick, his upper lip was covered in down. She caught his finger in her lips. He pulled away again.

"Are you biting me?"

Olya's eyes laughed to calm him, and she rubbed her tongue along his finger.

"You're tickling me," he said.

"Okay, I'll stop." She let him go. "Wait, I'll rub it off." She rubbed his mouth.

He didn't try to leave, but examined her closely.

"All right, you can go!"

He hunched his shoulders and left the room.

She spat the saliva from his mouth into her handkerchief, but the taste of cheap sweets and a pink after-taste of strawberry toffees lingered in her mouth. She wondered how to spin out the time until evening, when she could decide how to seduce the boy and play with him before they were caught.

Sea, sea, wash me white, wash me dead, wash my burning flesh, bleach my bones through and through, to the marrow, to the nerve.

There was a stout, elderly Jewish woman on the beach with her pretty little granddaughter, whose face was still hidden. The child wore knickers and a delicate handmade straw hat with flowers; cold, cherry eyes and a little golden body, babyishly clumsy. The old woman had bright red lips and a black plait wound around her head, and the bald patches of her scalp were stained black. In the canteen she grabbed everything, squeezing the pitta bread in her fingers and talking in a loud, piercing voice, revelling in the fact that everyone could hear her as she stood there with her black bathing-suit stretched over her noisy stomach. The ordinary people stood nakedly in the queue, wearily scratching their bare backs, too shy to tell her not to grab, but unable to take their eyes off the large grabbing woman and admiring her loudness. The granddaughter was bored. Haughtily sticking out her pretty lower lip, she hopped first on one leg, then the other, pulling down her knickers to scratch her white belly-button. The old woman broke through to the last piece of chicken, informing everyone that Olya was a usurper – how dare she steal her place and her chicken? Olya got a half-burnt sausage, like everyone else. As she took it, she tweaked the little girl's belly-button, and the child forgot to stare at her coldly from under her straw-hat and gawped at her in amazement. Olya grimaced, and the little girl gave a little smile not at all like a six-year-old's.

"I'm an idiot. I let that squit of a girl get the better of me – why do I get involved? I'll quietly eat my sausage, then go off and do my nails. Maybe I'll dream of the one who thinks about me at night, when I am alone."

She went on the beach with her manicured nails, her white skin.

"Hey miss, you'll burn."

"That's all right."

"Did you arrive today?"

"Maybe."

Oh, distant South of my childhood, come back to me. Remember weak bones, strong sea, happiness.

If you walk up the hill in the evening, the road is white in the darkness. Shining behind the hedge are places where people stay. Their words filter through the polished leaves and gently brush my cheeks. I like passing them as I climb up higher. They are fearless of death. They laugh about radiation with their drawn-out Ukrainian laugh. The splendid ship will sink later, when I am no longer I, and only my ring will reveal that this was she.

Down in the harbour she can see the ship. It sails in once a week, handsome and white-chested. Where it has been it will not say. Silent, gleaming and expensive, with quiet music wafting from its fragrant saloons. Those who bought tickets have a whole month to stay in the bright places behind the dark hedge. They laugh about radiation, their pink tickets tucked inside their purses. Ukrainian children in identical swimming-costumes file along the beach with their Pioneer leader.

"Hold on to your hats in the wind, children!"

The children hold on, bewitched by the sea.

"We fought the Turks for this sea. This sea is part of our country. Do you like the sea, children?"

"Yes, we like it!"

Every so often one of the children throws up in the sun, sick from not wearing a hat. "Don't make me go back, I just forgot my hat, that's all!" he says. But he is taken away, never to return. Saying goodbye to his friends, the pale boy looks longingly at the children and at the sea. He smiles, not understanding how you can say goodbye to the sea, how he won't exist any more. Here he is, looking at everything. When he stops he will fall into forgetfulness and not notice how he has gradually stopped being.

"The proud Ukrainian doesn't fear radiation!" say these world-famous children, blown by the sea winds. "It will be borne through the air and brought down by the wind, and we shall swim in the sea. Goodbye, Petro. Goodbye, boys. Take my hat. Give it to Mother."

I shall walk to the top of the hill, as far as the observation-platform. You can see everything from there. Frightening youths lurk in the darkness, wondering whether to pounce. Walk on slowly, ignore them howling behind your back, don't quicken your step. The road winds upwards, the houses disappear – a stone wall on one side, the ravine on the other, the path in the middle. Am I lost? But this is the only path. Now the wall ends, and it's open space again, a wilderness, a radio station encased in wire netting. Why do I imagine a mass of cockroaches behind the netting? It must be from childhood. The hottest grass lies behind that netting. A lot of people walk on it, because at the far end stands the radio-station, or whatever it is, guarded by beautiful blue netting. The grass is always best behind the shining fence. There are lots of crickets there, with cockroaches on top of them, as blue as the netting. You're not allowed in, you have to walk on just a little higher, to the top of the hill.

Here at last is the observation-platform. From here you can see the whole town, running down the hillside all the way to the sea, blinking and pulsing in the gleaming piles of the hotels and around the black gaps of the parks. You can't hear the town from up here. Slut-town, pining all winter, torn and ragged from the storms, counting the nights until the taut, youthful summer influx – what is this town to me? Why did I bring myself here? Why does it look like that up here? The naive lure of your grilled chickens and cream puddings, of dark Georgians selling plastic fishes, and shy Japanese mimosas shining in the heat. Here it's dark, you can't see the chickens or the mimosa – I am alone looking down on you. Observation-platforms were built so people could climb up and see how they live down below. They look for their houses, and the lucky ones pick theirs out from all the other identical houses. Look at our clump of garden down there, it's so much lusher than the rest, we live well in our garden.

I don't know how this sickness started in me, this sadness, muted but stubborn, this dread of every passing glance. I have lost my voice, I am afraid of other people's words, afraid of answering, afraid of saying the wrong thing. I try to listen to others, to imitate their words and learn from them how to speak, but I leave out some vital word and it all ends in disaster. I keep hoping it is nothing serious, but life gets harder and harder for me. I am afraid to enter a shop, pay out my money and take the goods, I am afraid to approach someone to ask the way. It's not just chicken that's out of my reach but the very rocks – even the grass here, I can't reach even that. I speak softly and am unable to ask for things. I have a lot of money, but it means nothing because I hand it over shyly, like leaves, and I am afraid to see what it buys. It's not just the rocks which are out of my reach but the air itself, because other people breathe it, noisy people, and I speak softly, and my voice has abandoned me, and I have grown thin. My skin won't go brown; burning hot in the sun and salt, it stays white, a dull, glassy white, only supple. The little girl from Makeevka announces loudly: "She's bad. We all go brown, but she stays white!" At the table swollen from the night rain people sit playing cards, and I am standing alone in the darkness on this observation-platform, looking for them in the town below, full of everything. Do I want to look at it? Not particularly – I shall go down and live the rest of my life.

She heard no sound, but realised from the movement of the air, a warm ripple down her back, that someone who had been hiding unnoticed for some time and observing her, had detached himself from the wall. He came up to her, leaning over beside her as she forgot to breathe.

"It's chilly here," he said.

At first there is this feeling of strangeness, like your illness, accumulating in the organism and drawing energy into itself, so you can't even get a sun-tan, it all goes inside. But your sadness is only impatience with the slowness of life. You test yourself out on different objects and people. Nothing comes of it, everything shrivels from your tentative touch, there is no one to play with. Now you're on your own at the top of the hill, higher and sadder than anyone. This is it, the final push, you're ready for something new. Everything different, unbearable for ordinary people, comes to you to play. So you wait.

Olya looked closely at the man. Limp hair above a balding forehead, two smile lines around the lips. As he looked down at the town with wide open eyes, she wondered if she had misheard. His face, dark from the sun, was calm, not coarse, he was just an ordinary passer-by. He stirred, then slowly moved his glance from the town towards Olya, and gradually revealed his face. A point-blank stare, like people who are not quite normal, cranks or artists, who stare like children into the heart of the eye. The town below sprawled gracefully in his eyes. Forgetting to be frightened, Olya looked until the picture sunk to the bottom of his eyes. Two little towns in two moist eyes – then they were gone.

"Do you like it up here?" a pleasant voice enquired. "Aren't you scared? Why do you walk alone at night to the top of the hill?"

"Not scared, just cold."

"All right, I believe you."

"It's a good thing you do, or I'd be upset!"

"I just thought you might have come out looking for adventures."

"No adventures, I just came out. There's nothing to stop anyone walking on this earth."

The man laughed kindly, they were warming to each other.

"In fact I am ill," she said. "Something keeps trembling inside me."

"I know what that is – neurasthenia."

"Neurasthenia is curable, in me the trembling goes deeper, where pills can't reach."

"Have you tried alcohol?"

"Alcohol makes me throw up."

"Brandy?"

"That too. Proper food makes me throw up, drink too…"

"So why did you come? People come here on holiday."

"Where else should I go?"

"Get a certificate to say you're crazy. I mean it – everybody has them these days."

"What would I do with it?"

"Just in case you get up to something."

"I'm frightened of people, don't you understand? That's why I creep off to dark places, to escape from my fear. I'm frightened of everyone, even Gala."

"Who's Gala?"

"The cashier at the hotel. She cheats everyone. You stand there gaping as she takes your money..."

"Bugger money."

"I do. Then I want to throw up. You must be crazy too if I can say all this to you."

"I've a certificate."

"So what's wrong with you?"

"Just mad, nothing serious."

"See, you're afraid to name it. That means the norm still tempts you. Why bother with a certificate? And why hang out here? Men can get done over too, you know."

"I know they can. I just needed a walk."

"I needed to let rip – to say murderous things to people. Do you understand?"

"You mean insulting people?"

"Maybe. Murderous things. I can't explain it – it's about letting rip, or else everything inside gets frozen and I want to throw up, as though there's nothing inside but puke. I want something to move inside me. If I really did someone over, everything inside me would be drowned in the blood of terror and compassion."

"Try to do me over."

"You wouldn't let me. Besides, you've already compromised yourself by talking to me."

"There's a lot of us around!"

"I thought it was only me."

"No fear, there are more and more of us!"

"It's even worse than I thought, then. I thought I could be crushed like a beetle, but if we're so many..."

"You know, maybe you're not so bad after all."

"When everything makes me throw up? I remember good and bad, they were names, it was so simple – but it was a long time ago, it's only the names I remember."

"For instance?"

"Well, peace on earth."

"You're like an illiterate person parroting the papers."

"And that people should be kind and polite... I don't

know, I don't remember. The main thing is that nothing bad should happen to us. I've lived a lot, I even have money, honest money too, I had Seryozha, lover and leader – everything you could want from life. Yet I'm in despair."

"Look, life has been hard on you, you came here, we talked. That's not nothing."

"For now, yes, you're right, thank you. But I'm afraid it won't be enough. I'll start to shake. There, I'm shaking, I must go. Goodbye."

"We could meet again if you like."

"What can you suggest? Let's say goodbye. I'll go now and live the rest of my life."

"You're nice, all the same. And I don't believe the shaking and puking – that's just neurasthenia."

"Only because you're close to it yourself, it makes you feel comfortable... With you I can speak from the voice of my body. It's still young and sweet, and it's the only voice I have. Yet I keep trembling inside, violently..."

Walking a little way down the hill to a clump of trees, she left the road, collapsed on to the prickly grass and lay there until the nausea passed, her temples quietened and the lewdness of their words left her blood.

She went home. The lamp was still burning in the yard. She was surprised they were still up.

"Hello! We're from just outside Gomel, we arrived this morning, but we've already caught the sun, especially Lena. Arrived recently yourself? You're white too."

"I'm white too. I never go brown."

"Take it easy, that's what I say. Lena's shoulders have caught the sun."

"Just outside Gomel, where would that be?"

"A little town, you don't know it. You know Gomel? We're here with our children, how about you?"

"I'm on my own."

"Lena will be out of the shower in a moment, her shoulders have caught the sun. My name's Anya, what's yours? I work in medicine, we all get holiday passes at work, but I wanted to come with Lena. They give us passes all the time now."

"Why?"

"They might as well, we live right near it. This year they moved us all out, then they moved us back again. The schoolchildren were all packed off to health resorts."

"Why just the schoolchildren?"

"The little ones stayed with their parents, and a few people were left behind to work. We have a meat-process-ing plant and an oil base there, you can't leave them. Lena's at the meat factory, I'm a sister at the hospital, in surgical casualty. Inside the compound, well, no one can work there – it's all top secret, people are sent in to work by the week or the month. They have no teachers, no doctors."

"Aren't you scared, Anya?"

"My husband's scared, but I don't know. We've had so many fractures in casualty this year."

"Why is that?"

"Strontium – it's settling in the bones. Arms and legs get broken, so they bring them in to us. My daughter's hair has started falling out. I don't know. We were all given dose-meters. We measured ourselves and the levels were right up, so we went to the town council and said, these doses are no good for our children. They just told us it was none of our business. 'You were given the instru-ments to measure with, that's all,' they said. You want some fruit jelly? I made it this morning."

"Yes, please."

"Lena will be out of the shower in a minute, she'll bring it. It's in our room."

Lena comes out. "Hello, my shoulders are burning."

"Anya tells me you caught the sun. You must rub cream on them."

"I have some strawberry cream – smell that, like real strawberries!"

Lena removes her dressing gown at the belt, a patient, childbearing body with broad stomach and suckled breasts.

"Where did you catch the sun?"

Lena turned her back. Wispy ringlets of hair fringed her neck.

"Rub there, Anya."

"May I do it? I know how."

"Thanks. Just there."

The cream smells of strawberries. Olya carefully touches the hot shoulders so as not to disturb the ringlets of hair.

"Pull up your hair."

"You can rub harder, I don't mind, it doesn't hurt."

"Is your hair naturally curly?"

"It's not curly, it's just from the sea."

"So you work at the meat-factory – is there a slaughter-house too?"

"Yes."

"Is it scary?"

"You get used to it. Some women have worked there twenty years. It's true they drink more than the rest."

"I don't know how you put up with it," said Anya.

"You get used to it. I personally can't stand the sight of blood – you have blood in your operating theatre.

"You're wrong there – they make an incision and immediately clamp the vessels shut. But you wade around in blood – you have to wear special boots!"

"It's different. You get used to it."

"I couldn't do your job."

"And I couldn't do yours."

"Okay, radiation levels are high, they measure every-thing with meters – so why don't they move you all out?"

"What about the factory? We couldn't abandon that."

"Or the oil base. Hey, I forgot the jelly! Bring it out, will you, Lena?"

Lena brought out a cup of thin fruit jelly.

"Try it, it's good, it has cherries and apples in it."

"It smells good," said Olya, putting the cup to her lips then moving it away. "Did you buy the fruit here?"

"No, we brought it with us."

"I... I've had a chill, I'll wait till it warms up."

"It wasn't in the fridge, it was standing in the room."

"I'll just let it warm up."

She ran to put the cup in her room. The nurse ran after her. They stood in the light, the nurse understood, dropped her eyes and silently went out.

Olya sat on her bunk holding the cup in her hands – the runny, dark-red jelly from the little town just outside Gomel, the nurse's eyes, the patient shoulders of her friend, the smell of strawberries. Olya suddenly broke into wild laughter. Something new in her voice frightened her as she drank the blackish viscous liquid. "They drink this stuff at wakes. That's good, they'll see I've drunk it. But it'll make no difference, by crack of dawn they'll have gone off me, just like all the others here."

Next morning she overslept and was the last on the beach. She watched a man trying to wind-surf, or rather falling in the water – the water being so much better than the air it kept luring in the man with his sail. Then she went to the café, where a boy in a white jacket served her a glass of raw egg yolk. In her clumsiness she tipped over the glass with the spoons. Frightened, she put on a stern expression, apologised, firmly replaced the spoons in the glass, then tipped them over again, the other side this time. The spoons scattered over the counter, smearing it with water. The boy laughed at her sweetly, without rancour, producing a clean spoon and looking at her with his youthful gaze as she sternly ate her egg. She very much liked the kind boy, although she did not show it.

She went to the park to grieve under a magnolia tree. The best bench was under the Gogol statue. Gogol stood amid the oleanders, pale, unable to see out as the sun tried vainly to penetrate the leaves. Only his long nose lived a little, its tip yellow with living flesh. Gogol himself was in a deep, almost perpetual sleep, tormented by torments inaccessible to us. Olya sat nearby grieving and dreaming, pale as a statue in the midst of the poisonous oleander flowers. She saw nothing in her dreams, just the spoons falling this way and that. In her fear she had dropped everything, and the childish waiter had sensed her fear and given her a clean spoon from his hidden supplies.

There's a glimpse of the sea, far off but you can still hear it – no, that's the leaves. There's a powerful smell, it takes your breath away, those are the poisonous oleander flowers. And Gogol can never escape from them? No, he cannot. He has been left here to be photographed by anyone who wishes. Rude health mocks at him, so thin and pale. They hold out their babies to embrace him. "Say hello to Uncle Gogol – smile, click! Aren't we pretty, sit up straight, pat him on the cheek. Goodbye Uncle, goodbye! Please Miss, where are the entertainments?"

"There, beyond the roses." (Go off to the room of laughter, louts.)

They go, leaving Gogol standing alone amongst the hot, poisonous flowers.

A little old man, peeping out from behind the roses, sidles up in cream trousers, brow raised exaltedly, an incorrigible ladies' man.

"May I take a seat?"

"Sure."

He is wildly refined, you can see at once he's a difficult old man – just sit down under Gogol and be still.

The old man admires his lightly-tinted, neatly-filed nails; he's that kind of old man.

"It's not true that coffee's bad for you," he announces. "Don't believe what they say, drink as much as you like!"

She considers this.

"I love getting up in the morning – I throw open the windows, let the air blow through the flat..."

"How much would you rent it for?"

"What do you mean? I'd rent it for nothing. Fresh air, make coffee, drink it by the window, first cigarette of the day..."

Olya felt a pang of envy. "But it's said to be bad for the heart and nerves."

"Rubbish! I'm still alive!"

"So you tell me."

To hide his senile peevishness he stroked his head, as though suddenly remembering something. "You should always do the things you like!" he says intimately.

She looks with interest at him sitting before her, a weak-toothed old man, inspired and passionate, the smoke wafting elegantly from his fine nostrils, with thoughts and opinions, a light sun-tan and handsome cuff-links, an obdurate old man, lachrymose and stupefied by the ever-lengthening chase after life, sitting neatly on the edge of another's youth, bewitched by the chase. But he is still alive and sunburnt, and his eyes bulge slightly with sclerosis, and he is sitting there on the bench while Gogol stands head and shoulders above him with nowhere to sit. Gogol is pale, his eyes are deep pits, he hides nothing, and everyone laughs at him as they pass, and pinches his nose to make them feel ticklish inside. But nobody pinches the old man's nose. Lie in the warm ditch, old man, spread out your legs, and...

"Coffee is good for you," insists the old man.

"It's good for you?"

"Yes, it is."

"Really good for you?"

"It certainly is!" he shouted, trying to move the conversation along. "I buy it in bulk, you know."

"In bulk?"

"Yes, in bulk — so it'll last."

"To last? In bulk?"

"I buy a kilo a time, and store it."

"A kilo of coffee?"

"You think that's too much?"

"A kilo?"

"For a connoisseur, an expert, that's nothing! You're laughing at me!"

"No, I'm not," says dull Olya, surprised.

"I put half a teaspoon of sugar in the coffee jug, do you understand? And three, no four spoonfuls of coffee."

"I understand."

Forgetting herself, Olya starts swaying and rubbing her

legs, anguished by the boredom of the conversation, wondering in which direction it would be most pleasant to turn it and pinch the old man's nose.

The old man gasps and stops talking, offended, shocked at the sight of her stroking herself.

"So what else do you love?" she asks lethargically.

His watery eyes dart here and there, catching the white Gogol at their outer corners.

"Culture – I love it! Books, poetry, novels, the lot. I have to read everything."

"What for?"

"Oh, that's a... a..."

"A secret?" she hazards, defeated.

"Sort of," the old man beams tenderly, conquering her, drawing her, young, shameless and empty, into his secret world.

"So what is your secret? Why do you have to know books and culture?"

"To broaden my horizons."

"And the secret?"

"I'm – an interrogator!" the old man shouts, trembling.

A melodious bird quivers in a plane tree, twitters some nonsense then falls asleep.

"Yes, yes, an interrogator. I noticed at once that you weren't like the other girls."

"That's for sure."

"There's something out of the ordinary about you, you're – unusual." His eyes pop again, as though prone to reveal frightening things to him.

"Yes, so many interrogations!"

The wizened, masterful old interrogator.

Just then some Germans shuffle past. They are dressed like the rest of us, meek and contented, but their speech pokes memories of Olya's little childhood fascist.

"You mean military work?"

"That too. But mainly spies – traitors to the mother-land."

Olya blinked, looking for the first time at the old man,

fresh, modest and unflinching beneath her stare.

"Where are they? Where do you find them, how do you – you know, identify them?"

"At work," he groaned.

"Are there lots of them?"

"I wouldn't want to darken your bright..."

"Soul?" Olya prompted.

"Not that, no, your holiday."

"Never mind my holiday!"

"All right – yes, lots. Satisfied?"

She looked at him again, long and hard, examining this creature thoroughly. The creature's eyes glinted metallically like door knobs, and for an instant her mouth was filled with the taste of metal.

"So tell me, how you identify them."

"Sweet girl, sweet girl, how little you know life!"

"God!" Olya said startled, "Can anyone know life?"

The old man laughed happily, and she saw his tongue, yellow with nicotine. "That's nice. You can know life if... if you spend years of your life conducting interrogations."

"I once conducted an interrogation..." Olya observed darkly.

"You have to keep on top of them. Exposing our country's traitors – that's the task."

"Would you mind telling me what being a traitor involved?"

"Involves, you mean," he corrected her, then whispered: "They're out there, they're at it all the time."

"What, even here?"

The interrogator wagged his head intimately at her, as he had when telling her you should always do the things you like.

"How could anyone betray anything here? There's nothing but the sea," said Olya indignantly.

"There are hundreds of them," he replied, "giving away our secrets to foreigners."

"For cash?"

"Sometimes it's cash, sometimes it's hatred."

"What secrets can there possibly be at the seaside?" she said wearily.

"You wouldn't understand," he said.

"So how do you catch them?"

"I don't, I interrogate them. I told you, I'm an interrogator."

"So you catch them, then you interrogate them, then what?"

"The bullet."

Olya gasped. "All of them?"

"It's not me, it's the ones who come afterwards," he reminded her.

"But what if not all of them are traitors?"

"They all are!" he snapped.

"But I just read in the paper that the police had convicted someone of murder and beaten him up and given him nine years – and he didn't even do it!"

"In the first place," nodded the interrogator impatiently, "it's the court that convicts – the police merely catch them..."

"What's the difference?" squealed Olya. "He was a young boy, beaten up, nine years in prison, and he's innocent!"

"He is guilty!" insisted the old man.

"Why?" Olya barely managed to whisper.

"I know how the man in the street views this acquittal. But just look at him – a young man, a bundle of instincts..."

"So?"

"Don't you see, it's nothing but – you know, sex!"

"Ah, so that's it! He's young, slender, his skin is soft, his stomach caves in, his collar bones stick out, girlish shoulders, swollen lips!"

"Guilty!" shrieked the old man. "Guilty!"

"How many of them, these traitors – I mean, what do they say when you interrogate them? Do they know they'll be shot?"

"They always come to me at the very end, often the

night before being shot. It's the final interrogation, you see."

"To say farewell?"

"Something like that."

"So you hope they'll tell you their most crucial secrets? But why should they? I don't get it."

"No, my girl, they don't tell us secrets."

"So what's it for?"

"For tears."

"Tears of repentance?"

"Yes."

"And – they cry?"

"Fairly often."

"And..." Olya grabbed his arm, "then you let them go?" She surreptitiously squeezed and tugged at his sleeve. "After tears you let them go?"

"Never!"

"So why tears?"

"I told you, for repentance."

"Why do you need the repentance of corpses? They're no longer any use to you."

"They're no longer any use, no," he conceded. "But they must be punished. They must be executed. For the sake of our successors."

"Our successors will remember you," said Olya.

"Why do you think my face is like this?"

"Like what?"

"I'm a young man, you know. This is just the way I look. My face has aged from all the shootings."

"So?" Olya twisted around angrily. "Does everyone without fail cry when they come to you?"

"Look at my face. Look at it. It has grown old from seeing so many people shot. It's not easy, you know."

In an instant she brought her thumb and index finger together in a claw, grabbed his nostrils and pulled his nose down, lower and lower, to the hot sandy path which wound through the roses, into the room of laughter. Not hurrying to straighten up, he froze on the ground to think about this new traitor to the motherland.

Wiping the interrogator's snot from her fingers, Olya stood up, walked off past Gogol, and glancing back briefly at the deathly sweat on the statue's plaster brow, she walked down the sandy path through the rose bushes.

On the beach, however, she found a completely different old man, a marvellous old Georgian with both legs amputated below the knee, sitting beside the sea. Olya wondered who would help him into the waves for a swim, and how. With his frame? The old man was laughing with some little boys. Burned by the sun, they were shouting in a strange language which whirled and flew up to the sky. The old man's grey hair was cropped short like a six-year-old's. The boys dipped him in the water, black Georgian grandchildren in black shorts, their narrow backs streaked with salt. Olya half-closed her eyes then opened them, and the old man was already in the sea. She was astonished how quickly they dragged and threw him into the blue water. He stood in it up to his shoulders, wisely holding out his arms so as not to fall. On dry land, leaning on his frame, he submitted to his body's weight, but the water bore him up and his body laughed with happiness. The old man turned the back of his small firm head to us and scanned the line of the shore with eyes as black as those of the boys. His strong, handsome arms flapped and chopped at the waves, his shoulder blades stuck out of the water and he launched into a fine, even swimming stroke, playing with the air and the waves. He returned in disarray. In an instant he lost his balance, clumsily beating the water with his palms, struggling to keep afloat. Again the sea bore up her favourite, and he stroked her surface. The boys had run off long ago. How would he get out? He lay down again like a child, waiting for the little waves to wash him up to the dry stones. Grabbing hold of them with two hands and a leg, he clung to the ground, then scuttled faster than a two-legged person to his frame and settled himself in it, light, free and comfortable in his hot, dark body. Behold the happy mountain man, not full-sized, smooth and lovely as a sea pebble! Good, clever old man! He loves meat and wine, he has forgiven his frame.

Stretch out on the shingle, let your body grow used to the stones. The sun will spread over your body, don't move, or it will crush you. Slowly, gently reach for a stone, black with a stripe, cool it in your fingers, round and smooth, it fits in your palm, put it on your ribs where it's beating. During the day it absorbed the heat, it rolled in the sea before you existed, it contains everything you need for life, even better than food for the journey. Put it on your skin, where it's banging under the ribs, and draw healing energy from it. It is very simple. It understands only what is important.

I shall go quietly to my hut on the hill, wrap myself in white sheets, turn into a cocoon and listen to what is happening in me. How is life inside, warmed by the day?

But first to get past the table, the evening card-game.

"Good evening."

"Well, look who's here!"

"Where's Kostya?"

"Here I am – I've beaten everyone!"

"Serves them right!"

Black Gala left the table and flung her cards on the ground. Her mother said: "Now Gala, you'll win next time."

"Tell her to go away, then!" Gala commanded.

"I'm going," said Olya nervously. "Go on playing your Fool, Gala."

Kostya skipped from the table and took Olya's arm.

"The minute she comes we stop playing!" black Gala pointed at her.

"Gala, Gala," soothed her mother, "what pale hair you have. Do you want a nice story?"

"A scary one!"

"Okay, a scary one!"

"Do you want to come up and see my trains?" said Kostya.

"I'm a guest," said Olya. "I'm not allowed in your mum's house."

"You are with me! Mum, I'm going up to show Miss Olya my trains!"

"Go ahead!" rang from the depths of the house.

"See? Come, this way."

His room was covered in rugs, with a dear little bed under the window.

"Where's your table?"

"What do I need a table for? I eat with Mum, in the dining room."

"Your window looks straight over the ravine."

"So?"

"Aren't you afraid? I mean at night?"

"At night it's dark."

"And in winter, when the wind's blowing? Aren't you afraid then?"

"Nah, I get into bed with Mum, it can blow as hard as it likes."

"You sleep with your mum? In the same bed?"

"I hug her to stop her head aching in the wind, then we both fall asleep."

"Mum's head aches in the wind?"

"It's the noise. Then she got sick at the factory. She used to work at the factory. All they do is bury people at that place! The noise did something to Mum's head. She started aching and shouting – they gave her pills, but she wouldn't take them. She's right! They should do something about the noise instead!"

From behind the wall his mother called: "Kostya, what are you talking about in there?"

"I was saying they did something to your head!"

"Don't say such things!"

"So where are your trains?" said Olya loudly.

"In this box. Here, let's put the tracks together."

"Let's."

They put the tracks together.

"Now the carriages. Here, I'll do it!"

"And the signal-box?"

"All aboard! Here it is!"

"Wait, it's red!"

"You don't understand – we must go! All aboard, next station, Sochi!"

"Wait, I was late!"

"We can't wait. Catch us up on a plane!"

"Z-zzzz... Hurrah, here's a seat! We made it! Off we go!"

"Next station, Sochi!"

Gala came in.

"We're boiling up those tendril things off the mussel-shells. Come and see, Kostya!"

"Don't go Kostya, they stink!"

Kostya said: "I'm not going – I've seen them a hundred times."

"I'm going to play," said Gala.

"Go and play, Gala," said Olya.

"Let her go, then I'll play."

"Certainly not," snapped Olya, "go yourself."

"How can you, she's only little!" said Kostya in surprise. "She needs to play."

"Fine, you play with her."

"I will! Let's go! Next station, Sochi!"

At night in her cabin she heard him get up and go to the bathroom. Switching on the light she lay there as he scratched at her door.

"Come in."

"You're alone and you can't sleep," he said.

"Lie down with me, then I'll sleep."

"Mum will be looking for me."

"My head is aching."

"Is it bad?"

"Yes."

He was upset, stamping about barefoot in his pants, not knowing what to do.

"I'll put out the light and your Mum won't know."

She got up and switched off the light, then took his hand and pulled him to her.

"They'll shout at us," said the boy.

"No, they won't," she said.

"They'll shout at you anyway."

"That doesn't matter."

He put his arms around her neck.

"My headache will go in a minute."

Immediately he was asleep.

She lay quietly so as not to disturb him, then gently moved his arm from her neck so she could breathe, and lay guarding him as he slept, his breath tickling her neck. She moved slightly away from him; his body was burning, he had stayed too long in the sea and had a chill. He cried in his sleep and grabbed hold of her, astonishingly hard. She did not move again after that.

She awoke at dawn, not knowing if it was a thunderstorm or a landslide, or they were falling down the ravine, with the house balanced above the abyss and people risking their lives to rescue their things. Stirring, she saw a strange boy asleep beside her, his mouth half-open, trembling from the effort of sleeping. Strange how pale he was – a southern child, yet he was a pale, almost greenish colour.

"My little boy! My baby! Your little bed is cold!"

Olya looked at her watch: it was half-past four.

"Wake up Kostya! Everyone's looking for you!"

"Maybe he's run away?"

"Where would he run to at five in the morning? The child has been stolen! People have been prowling around!"

"We must keep looking! Perhaps he's in the bathroom."

"He's gone! Animals! You've torn out my heart! Take my money, take everything, just give me my child!"

"Wake up, Kostya! Wake up!" Olya pinched him angrily. The whole street was awake, only he was asleep.

"Give me back his dead body! Anything that's left of him – here's gold, just a hair from his head!"

"Kostya, what am I to do with you! Wake up at once!"

Suddenly everything went quiet, and she realised that people were looking in at them. She closed her eyes.

"They're sleeping. Together. He's safe."

"My God! Let go of me!"

"Steady on, don't rush in, they're not going anywhere."

"Mum, I'm not asleep! I was hiding here waiting for you to find me!"

"Poor baby! You're trouble, just like your dad! Come out, you whore! Show us your face! How dare you sleep with my boy! Come with me now, son."

"No, Mum, you'll only fight."

"You bet I will!"

"And Olya has a headache."

"Bitch, I'll kill her!"

"But she's still asleep," Kostya sobbed.

"Let her open her eyes, then!"

Olya opened her eyes.

"I won't kill you. The child's alive, that's enough. Don't look at me like that, I'm being nice, I'm not even going to hit you."

They tied Olya up.

"And I thought she was playing trains with him."

"Hey, what's the point of tying her up? There's lots of us, we can take her as she is."

They started to untie her, losing their temper and punching her a couple of times because they had made the knots too tight and couldn't loosen them.

"Look at her refusing to speak! She just stares at us!"

"So what did she do, then? What shall we tell the police?"

"She slept with this kid here. Well, let them sort it out."

They took her off.

"Goodbye, Kostya!"

"Take the signal-box!"

"I'll give you signal-box! Don't you dare say goodbye to him!"

She looked around in farewell and saw the woman who

had given her the fruit jelly. The woman's eyes gazed at her like a child gazing at a butterfly, and she remembered the smell of strawberries and the burning shoulders of the woman's friend.

They led her off to the police station, but half way there they changed their minds and headed for the beach, leaving only Gala, black and trembling with anger, to haul her to the police. Finally Gala was dragged away, silent with rage, kicking herself for failing to put Olya in jail.

I am often bored, but fear is always interesting to live with.

After going to the harbour toilets to change, Olya decided to do without a bed.

She walked out to watch the ships, saw that they had opened the Rotonda café and thought she would have a coffee. Then she remembered that the bag with her money was in the hut. She went back, tried to remember the code, and while doing so twisted the handle and the door fell open to reveal that everything had been stolen, except what she had on her – fifty kopecks and the bag with her bathing-suit. She walked back to the harbour, where the ship was standing there all white. The sailors looked down, Olya looked up.

She went to the Rotonda.

"A Greek coffee, please."

"Fifty kopecks."

The Greek dug the tin coffee-jug into the hot grounds. The Greek was hot; his after-shave smelt acrid. Olya took her coffee into a round tower-room. The acrid-smelling Greek followed her and turned up the music a little.

"Been on the beach?" he nodded at the bag with her bathing-suit.

She nodded back.

"Plunged in, did you?"

"Why?"

"Your cheeks are peeling."

"I'm a bad swimmer."

"Be careful, there's mussels on those stones," he went

on, "and they're sharp as razors."

"I know," Olya told the Greek. "Thank you."

Seated at the table next to her was a woman with her
twelve-year-old daughter and two young men. The girl was
bored and wet from the sea. They wouldn't give her coffee
because it was too early, and had bought her sweets
instead. She unwrapped them, removed the foil and twisted
it around her fingers. The elder of the two young men
looked at the girl's fingers.

"You like my fingers?" she asked capriciously.

"Cool," said the young man, "very flashy."

"Look at your nails!" gasped her mother.

"Scared?" the girl demanded, silver knives poised.

Abashed by her beautiful daughter, the mother flinched
away from the nails.

"Take them off!"

"No, I'm fed up."

"Go and play, then. Look, there's another girl!"

"What are you saying!" said the elder of the two young
men in alarm.

Tired of flirting with the young men, the beauty with
the nails aimed her silvery fingers at the chest of the
newcomer, a plump, bare-foot little Armenian girl.
Gasping, the girl laughed and ran towards them, twittering
and shrieking and shuffling her tiny heels. The elder young
man turned slightly away.

"What is your name, little girl?" asked the beauty's
mother.

"Layla. I want some too!" She stretched out her
rippling, boneless fingers.

The elder young man closed his eyes and hunched his
shoulders as Layla reached up over him, so he couldn't
move away. He was worried she might smell of fish, but
she smelt of nothing, just hot sand.

"Please can I have one?" she stretched out her finger
entreatingly.

The beauty frowned slightly, then accepted the
inevitable, removed one nail from her graceful little finger

and stuck it on Layla's thumb.

"Give me more!"

"No more!" The beauty was selfish.

"It's not enough!"

"All right then." One by one the beauty unwrapped four more sweets and spread the foil on Layla's fingers. Layla gasped again – now she was all shining too. Each time the beauty touched the plump little girl the elder of the two young men winced, even though he was pinned by her plump body to the back of his chair.

"How nicely they play together," said the mother. "What class are you in, little girl?"

Layla tensed, dropped her long eyes comprehendingly, and sensed that everything was all right.

"Year three."

The mother was anxious, looking surreptitiously at Layla as the beauty explained passionately how to make silver fingers. The young men were silent. Needing more space, the girls jumped up and ran from the grown-ups, laughing and waving their fingers. Still laughing, they ran outside. The sailors looked down at the silvery girls. Glancing distantly at them, Layla's Russian mother passed, carrying a tray of dirty cups. Olya managed to add her empty cup to the tray and wandered into the heat.

The little girls laughed and waved their fingers as the beauty shrieked and hiccoughed helplessly with laughter. "Fingers, fingers!" screamed Layla, unable to believe her eyes.

"Ooh, ooh, ooh!" hooted the beauty, her white dress fluttering over her knees. The sailors looked down at the girls from the white ship. The strip of water between the mooring and the ship looked up, and trembling spots fell from its glance to the white decks above. The girls did not see the sailors as they laughed and played with their silvery sparks of light. The ship breathed quietly, rocking the sailors above, ducking away from the shiny girls towards the even sea. The sailors were young, they looked down at the girls. The little girls played like steel knives and laughed like glass. The water could not move the ship – it was one with the young sailors, it traced faint spots of silver, painting depths on the dry upper decks.

The girls were small and soon tired of laughing. The beauty peeled off her nails, the Armenian hid hers behind her back, for fear that they would take her silver away. The beauty looked at the Armenian with sad, wise little eyes. A breeze fanned her white dress over her teenager's knees. On her left knee a young scratch had flowered.

"I'm off," said the owner of the dress and the scratch. "Mum gets lonely on her own with her boyfriends."

"Who are her boyfriends?"

"Oh, they follow us around everywhere so we won't be bored. Mum helps them with their work."

"Will we play again?"

"You can have my nails if you like. I don't need them any more."

"Will you be staying here?"

"Don't expect so," the beauty looked around distractedly. "We never stay anywhere, we get bored. See, this is how you do it – twist the silver paper and stick it here, over your nail."

"The silver?"

"That's right. Bye now."

"Bye."

It was boring now. The beauty ran off. The plump barefoot girl stood alone in her sun-bleached beach-robe, awkwardly flashing her silver hands. The sailors turned away from the shore. The ship rocked and rocked them on the even sea.

At night the sun-beds on the beach are still warm. I could go to the station, of course. If I can't sleep here, I'll go to the station. The taste of coffee lingers on, and the silvery girls... but that was a long time ago. Now it's the empty sea, the frozen beach. The little white chairs in the café above are visible in the darkness with their elegantly curved backs. I could sit there, it's all mine now.

Olya sat on a chair. Was she hungry? She had had nothing all day but water from public drinking-fountains and a bite from a child's roll. The café looked at Olya and was silent. The little white chairs surrounding the empty tables slowly released the warmth from their daytime seats. Olya wanted to sleep, she felt slightly sick from hunger. Pushing the chair back to the table, she walked down to the beach again, stretched out on a sun-bed and waited for sleep, the bag with the swimming-costume under her head. The sky was alive with deep, heavy movements. Olya breathed. The sea lay quietly, whispering a little. Olya thought about the dog. Closing her eyes, she tried to compare and decide what she should do, but the dog kept getting in the way. She should be thinking about herself, but the dog proved stronger.

All right, I'll think about you, she decided. You frightened me, but it wasn't you, it was death appearing through you. You came to us in December, a little red dog freezing on our doorstep, and I took pity on you. We'll light the stove and you can lie there to die, I thought. I called you, but you wouldn't come, looking at us through your pain with the last drop of trust gone. Yet trust us you did. Thinking we might have medicines, you came in, staggering and scratching the floor. I didn't see that you were bleeding. You lay down by the stove and stayed there, and I thought you would live, but you just drank some water and went out again into the snow. Back in the room, you passed a red stream of water. At first I cried, but once it was obvious you wouldn't eat I shouted at you. When I picked up the food, you lifted your face and watched me carry it away, and even that small movement of life was cause for joy. We started waiting for you to die. Knowing this, you staggered out again, claws scratching the floor, to pour more red water into the snow. I wondered about the person who had killed you.

You returned to the dry place by the stove. On the cold verandah there was a gas cooker, and I decided to make soup and give you the broth, to nourish you and bring you

back to life by deceiving you that it was water. If you
recovered I would love you at once. Later I would tell
everyone: this is my dog, I healed her wounds, I bath her,
she sleeps on the sofa, she's got over her shyness, she's
spoilt, she's not a stray any more. I opened the verandah
door to look at the soup, then quickly closed it again so as
not to let in the cold. You stood up suddenly, and crawled
to the door, groaning and falling. I let you out and you
collapsed on the cold verandah, where the soup was
cooking in a cloud of steam. You lay there, howled
strangely about far-off things and scratched the linoleum. I
was frightened and closed the door against you. The soup
started to boil, but I just watched it through a crack in the
door, not daring to rest my eyes on you. You saw me and
tried to crawl to me, thinking that because I had opened
the door to you before, I would let you in again. You
thought if you came in you would not die. But I did not
let you in, I just waited for it to end. I managed to put my
hand out and lift the lid of the saucepan so the soup was
saved. When I looked out, you crawled towards me
begging to be let in. As the soup was cooking, you were
dying. You grew huge and black and frightening. The soup
cooked. My husband was not back. There were three of us
in the snow – you, me and our soup. You died, the soup
cooked. I stepped over you and carried it inside, terrified
that you would move. You lay in the puddle of your last
blood. My husband came back, and I said: she's dead, take
her away. He didn't know what to do. He lifted her up by
her front paws and dragged her out, her head flung back
and her breast all white. She was a small dog, but in his
torment she seemed large and heavy.

He carried her to the end of the empty cul-de-sac,
where nobody went, and he laid her neatly in the snowy
ditch. A red dog with a white breast. The breeze ruffled
the white fur on her breast, her sweet mongrel face. Two
weeks you lived with us, and you chose that night to die.
We went back into the house, where it was already bright.
The terrible moment had passed. We sat down and ate our

soup. Nobody came and asked: "Who killed the dog?" She could lie out in the snow, her soft fur growing cold, and no one would ever ask about her. Yet who was it who prolonged her death? We ate our soup, cooked in the cloud of death. If we had been better off, we might have poured it away, but soup was a luxury for us in those days.

I am astonished by how hungry I was then. Today I have had nothing but a distant cup of coffee and a bite from a roll, and I am neither hungry nor thirsty. But something has to be done. I'll go shouting and weeping to the police-station – maybe they'll feed me. To look into others' faces, to speak words, the voice from the body. Still, it's good to know the police are there. They'll think of something.

So she thought about the dog, and she thought about herself, although it would be better to think about nothing. Then, for the first time in years, she felt surprised, and sitting up on her sun-bed she looked around the beach, gazed far away at the sea, and thought: I can start now. My own shameless crime was in the eyes of that little red dog. Now I've thought about her and taken her out of her hiding-places over the years – and all along it was *me* I was thinking about. I could think about the boy, sleeping over the abyss, but I'm afraid he has probably had a good hiding and forgotten all about me. This is it – no need to think any more, just stop. Everything has been stolen from me, anyway. I could put energy into getting myself out of this mess, but the fact is I don't have the energy, just like with the red dog. I took pity on her, I devoted energy to her, but it proved to be a dream, and I didn't even know how to wash her wounds, how to find them in that thick coat, or reach them through her snarling brown tangle of flesh and fur. Okay, so I'll think about my goldfish when I was a child...

She lay back slowly on her hard sun-bed and closed her eyes, hoping that after thinking about the fish she would stop thinking altogether. But the goldfish were jumping out of their bowl – she had put in too much water and not left enough space for air. Little Olya watched the fish quivering on the desk. She could not pick them up for she didn't know where they hurt, but this was the first time she had seen fish on the writing desk, and she couldn't tear herself away. When all the fish had jumped out and were hopping about on the desk, her mother came in and said, "If you'd poured out some water they wouldn't have died."

"But I had no time..."

"You had time ten times over."

"I loved them so much!"

"You couldn't have loved them if you let them die!"

The sharp air cut through their little fins and burned up their wet intestines. No, it was no good, fish weren't fluffy and didn't groan, so you couldn't feel sorry for them. I'll just lie here without regrets, and think about the most obvious things – the sun-bed is hard, the sea air is cold. It's impossible to stop thinking altogether, because the body and its voice keep muttering about what is happening to them. I could get up and watch the sea. The sea's body is far greater and more ancient than mine. But I'm lazy. Or I could just open my eyes, that's not hard. When I close my eyes the world seems to grow more beautiful without me. I open them and see a man.

"You no sleep?" says the man, watching me with black eyes. "Why you lie here all alone?"

The man's blind life stares out stubbornly from his eyes. "You want to go restaurant? Why you lie here?"

The trembling man burns with greedy life. "I talking to you, woman! Why you lie here? What you looking at?"

Life can't go on, and wrenches itself from the man's dark body.

"Bitch!" he screams, and unable to find more words he starts yelling obscenities at her in his resonant language. Then he grabs the bag with the swimming-costume from under her head, weighs it in his hand, and shouting more obscenities, he takes it and goes off to live his life.

She falls asleep instantly.

So, the South. A piece of glass flashed beautifully. She picked it up and walked along, feeling contented and wanting to sleep. Two barefoot girls in long shirts played in the water, clambering on to the breakwaters, pushing each other off and falling back in the water. She laughed too, wanting to join them, but there was nowhere to put the glass. She searched her dress – nowhere. Then looking around, she cunningly buried it in the shingle and waded laughing across the water to the girls.

The air was light and bright. Olya made her way over the rocks towards the girls. The rocks were silky, clad in short weed. She stroked the weed, the weed stroked her legs. One girl splashed the water nearby, about to jump in again. The other, quicker girl stood on a rock guarding her friend. Olya stepped over to another stone. The second girl pushed the quick girl into the water and they both fell in, clutching the air with their hands. She waited for them on the stone. The girls jumped about in the water, holding hands. They climbed out and plunged in again, shirts clinging to them as they clambered out and jumped in, beating the water white.

Olya went in deeper. Shrieking, they beat their heels, swum away from each other and leapt up in the air. Tired of following the girls, Olya sat on a gentle rock and looked around to see who was lost. The water billowed her skirt over her knees, the weed on the stone stroked her feet, sharp mussels poked from the weed, everything was cheerful and in its place. Frozen, she headed back to the shore, stretched out and lay there.

She walked, looked, slept. Everyone was cheerful. Life was good.

Towards evening she grew uneasy. Everyone went off, and she was alone. She slept by the water, a dog came up and lay beside her, warming her. In the morning everyone came back. She was happy, followed them, looked.

She walked and walked, and came to a place where there were lots of people. It was crowded and delicious-smelling, with birds and fruits and people standing behind them. Everything was red and black from the fruit. She took a soft juicy berry, and an old woman sighed and nodded at her to go ahead and take one. She nodded back and saw a wooden doll, lots of dolls shining at her. Nobody touched the dolls. The dolls smiled. She didn't dare touch one, she just stood staring and chewing a peach, her fingers sticky with the juice.

"Buy a doll, buy a glass – look, it's decorated with flowers. See this jar of berries, you could put anything in it!"

The dolls smiled, their black eyes silent. She saw some blackberries and took one in her fingers. The berry wept red, she dropped it and licked her fingers.

"Here, eat some bread."

She took the bread. It warmed her mouth, she wanted to lie down by the water with it warming her mouth. But she ate the soft dough as the berries wept capriciously in her hands. Then she went to watch the birds, walking past the dolls and smiling at them. The birds sat on their own, wanting to be quiet.

"Hey, give that one something to eat, but mind it's not meat."

"Give her some of your lamb pie, what's left of it. Don't worry, she won't mind meat."

"She will. They're sensitive."

"Give her milky coffee, then. You've some left."

She drank. It was sweet and warm in her mouth.

She walked on. Dangling brightly in a dark hand was a big bunch of grapes. The hand pulled at the vine, the grapes dreamed on by themselves. She grasped the bunch in her hand and took a good look. There was a terrible bellowing and beating, and grapes scattered from the branch.

"He gone! He gone away!"

Hands beating, a black mouth shouting, large hands grabbing at her.

"Where are grapes? Where are grapes? You eat him?"

She looked around her in fear. Strange hands barred her

way, tearing at her face and body.

"Where he gone? Where you put him? What you looking at?"

Slipping over the grapes, she tried to tear herself from the hands. Somebody was lost!

"Where he? Where he?"

Her face burned from the strangers' hands.

"Where he gone? You tell us!"

Somebody was lost! Who were they looking for? She must break away and look for him!

"Where? Where?"

She tried to pull away, to run in search for him. The hands wouldn't let her, she struggled, they burned harder, she struggled harder.

"Where?"

She started shouting. Silence fell. You could hear where he had gone. The hands slipped away and let her go. Silence. Everyone breathed together. A bird stirred. The bird disappeared. Silence, silence. He was not lost, he was hiding somewhere nearby. She started to look.

"Go! Go! You no come back!"

He was over there. She could hear him. She must go after him!

She looked and looked. He was nowhere. She grew desperate.

"Who tore your dress all over, you poor thing?"

She saw black hands and frowned. The hands went away.

"Here, get this egg down you. Don't look at it, silly, eat it! That's right, crack it and drink it. Better? What were you crying about, eh?"

It had been good, now it was bad. She must go, go, faster, too slow, run faster! She ran and ran. It grew dark. She stopped. Everyone had gone. She knew it would be light and they would come back. She would find him and everyone would see he was back. She looked at her finger where the ring had been, and her hand was empty. Someone was weeping inside her chest. She rubbed her chest with her empty hand. She wanted to sleep but sleep was impossible, she must look for what was lost. A flame flickered in the air. Floating and breathing, it settled on her hand, crept from the empty place on her hand to her fingers, then flew into the dark air.

Someone was weeping inside her chest, under her ribs. A strong wind came up, and she knew she must go to the big water. But the sea was breaking for the shore. Howling, terrible, heaving itself up from its depths, it bore itself on and on, howling to the land, for he was lost. Howling and breaking, it wounded itself on the stones of earth, but would not go back. The heavens roared and fell in the water, beating it with fire. Power was everywhere, water was everywhere. The fire sank. The shattered sky roared. Power had no place and fell back. It was impossible to live. There was no light. Power roared and devoured the light. Power left the body of the earth, the water, the air. Leaping and lurching in the air, power went inwards. Growling, she ran with the power, and the shattered sky responded. Strong! Impossible to live! Happy after life! He is nowhere! He is lost!

Something warm brushed her leg. Stumbling, she bent down to discover who was still warm after life, and saw it was the dog again, pressing against her. She growled to the dog about power. The dog laid its muzzle on her knee and trembled. She was surprised to see the dog was still warm after life. Trembling and powerless with power, it didn't want to fly and howl. She pushed it away so it would not see how frightened she was, but it clung trembling to her legs and wouldn't go. It had come to look at power, but it could not. She showed the dog her hand, and the power roaring inside it. The dog looked, the fire died down, then flared up, the dog sank on to its paws and summoned her away. Yes, go! Power blew into her chest under the bones, nobody was crying now. The dog moved off. Now she must breathe with power! The dog waited alone, not powerful, not cold. The dog was living, it didn't know life was already over. She followed the dog. They walked, striking the air and the water, and went down the steps of a little jetty under which boats were moored. They crawled and squeezed through a tight hole, then lay down and looked through the boards at the water tugging the boats. The water lapped at their stomachs as they lay looking down. The boats creaked, the water snarled. She felt cold and turned to the dog. The dog growled, laid its muzzle on its paws and let her move closer. The dog warmed her. She lay listening to it wheezing. It was warm. The skies lifted, the boats fell asleep, the water was tired, everyone slept, the dog yelped in its sleep. She touched it to stop it trembling. It was warm, everyone slept.

The sky was blue and silent, its light burned her face and shoulders. Walking was difficult. Everyone was lying quietly beside the silent water, which gave off light. She walked on, looking for food. The grass called her. She walked across it remembering the water, but it was still a long way off. She stretched out on the grass, the grass whispered, creatures crept out of it, crawling and flying about – one whirred over her face. She turned and saw a plum lying where there wasn't much grass. The plum was hot and alone, its skin had burst and was oozing bubbles of hot juice and sugar. It was very shiny. It was out of her reach. It lay there waiting. It was better to wait.

They were slipping and crawling all over the plum. It made you want to laugh and look at it lying on the ground, oozing bubbles of juice and sugar.

A little snake ran up on short legs and opened its mouth. The snake was grey, its mouth was yellow. It gobbled some of the plum and swallowed. Another snake ran up, a young one, and swallowed hard. The grey one pushed off the young one, which ran away gulping, then more snakes came up and started eating.

"Hey, you can't lie there! You hear me?"

The grey snake pushed away the others and thrust its head into the plum. The rest pushed and trembled and lashed their tails and crept back into the plum, then ran off gulping. At last they all left.

"Get up, you hear me?"

The empty plum lay there.

"Get up off the grass!"

"Leave her be, can't you see she's whacko?"

"There's tourists here, they'll see her!"

She lay there shining, and watched through the empty hole.

Everyone had eaten and gone, but the empty plum remained. She lay and waited. She must get up and go to it. She picked up the empty plum. It smelt hot. She started chewing.

"Look, she's eating grass!"

"That's not grass, it's something she found in the grass."

She delayed swallowing, because she wanted to make her saliva sweet. She touched the bit of ground where she had lain. Snakes were asleep on the stones, creatures crawled and flew around. Her saliva was still sweet. There was no more plum left, just a lot of full snakes and sweet saliva. It was good to be alive, the sun was hot. Someone looked straight into her head. He spoke gentle words. "Go and look for warm bread, they'll give you some, it doesn't lie there like the plum." She did not know she was afraid (she remembered the grapes), she thought she wanted to lie in the grass, but she wanted warm bread.

She went to where the ships were. They stood quietly, very large, wanting to come in. Earth could not hold them, water could. They made your eyes ache, they were so clean, living always in the water. They waited and watched, but they were driven back. They roamed across to the edge of the big water, then disappeared from sight. That is where they lived. But still they wanted to come in. It was cheerful down by the ships, there might be bread there. She walked and waited.

Down on the ground by people's feet, she saw the little man with the frame, supporting himself on the ground with his arms. A bottle stood beside him and he drank from it. Beside the bottle lay a small piece of bread. The little man looked ahead of him at the big water, but the ships were in his way. He rocked angrily from side to side, beating his fists on the ground. Then he picked up the bottle and drank from it, irritably took a bite of his bread and looked out at the big water. His back was wet with heat, his hair was warm with life. She went up to the man and touched his hair. It responded to her touch. She kneeled beside him. His voice rang out. She kneeled and looked at his responsive hair. She felt awkward kneeling, but she didn't want to stand up and leave him. He held the bottle, drank from it and passed it to her. A smell of bread came from the bottle. She took a sip and wiped her lips. He showed his teeth. She laughed at his laughter. They both looked at the water, it was full of light. The man drank from the foaming bottle, there was a smell of bread and water.

"Can't you speak, then?" he asked.

Foam crept out of the bottle. He licked it off. "Not much. See, I'm all cut off outside. It's different for different people. With you it's all inside – there's nothing there."

The man was short, his legs thrust down into the ground. Resting his fists on the ground, he stared at her some more. "Who do you live with? I'm on my own."

The man's voice wanted to fly but it was afraid, and hid itself in a hot whisper. If it flew away he would be alone, without legs or voice.

"I'm thirty-two years old. My arms are strong. I can do lots of things."

If his voice went away, he would be unable to hold on to the earth, and it would drag him down by his warm hair.

"Which of us is worse off? What does a woman need a brain for anyway, or a voice? All she needs is legs and a face. I can do anything – I can go anywhere, I can swim..."

His voice deceived him and he knew it, grabbing his bottle and biting off more bread.

"At home I do everything myself. I bet you don't even have a home with that ring on your finger, no stone on it or anything."

More people came up. Their tallness startled her. She looked up and saw four black nostrils. From such a height their eyes looked frightened, as though they didn't know what to do next. Their voices spoke to the small man.

"Hey Tolik, found yourself a girlfriend?"

"Sure have, Dima. She sat down and she isn't going!"

"She's got the lot, eh?"

"Can't argue with that. You want a swim?"

"You going to marry our Tolik, love?"

"She can't speak. Want to go to the pictures?"

"No point talking to her, you don't need words to do it."

"Want to come swimming with me, love? What you looking at me for? Hey Tolik, she nicked your bread!"

"Let her!"

"Give it back to him! You should ask first!"

"She can't speak!"

"She's lying! I heard her talk!"

"Can't you see she's a fruitcake? Tell him, Dima!"

"Let her tell us herself that she's a fruitcake, then she can have the bread! Go on, tell us you're a fruitcake!"

"You better go now, girl, the lads are angry. Go on, take the bread and scram."

He beat his fists on the ground. Someone was lost!

"She's left the bread! Hey, take the bread!"

"You'll never catch her up, Tolik. Come on, Dima!"

To be saved, one must endure. They cut out my pancreas, and I was in pain. I couldn't eat, I had no strength. Then they discovered they had to do another operation. That was three operations. They cut me to pieces. After that I walked around the city and thought, how much longer do I have? How long can a person live without their pancreas? I see people strolling about, just like before – children, too – the sun's lovely and hot. I'll die, I thought, the earth will close over my head, and everything will be exactly the same as it was before. No one will notice that old Valya is

gone. So if it's inevitable, why is my heart so heavy? Am I
sad that I won't be seeing all these strangers any more? My
own son has forgotten me and gone off without leaving an
address. Am I sad for life? But my time must come, it's the
same for everyone, it's a law of nature.

Autumn is coming and I see a rowan-tree, and standing
beside it a young old man in boots. He is all covered with
dust from the road, and on his back is a bag on a string.
The old man stands and looks at the rowan-tree quivering
– there were a lot of rowans that summer and it's weighed
down with red bunches. I stand there looking at the two of
them, and I think he's going to ask me why I'm staring at
him without asking. I know it's wrong to stare, but I can't
look away, something about him amazes me. When he sees
I'm not going, he turns to me, his face all serious, and he
says: "Happy holiday to you!" And I say: "Which holiday
would that be?" And he looks at me again, as though he's
sorry he spoke, and he doesn't reply. And I say: "Tell me
which holiday you mean, citizen." And he sees I'm not
going, he thinks a bit, then he decides he doesn't mind,
and he says: "The Holy Birthday." I'm surprised again in
spite of him, because I know Christmas comes in winter.
Then he says: "The birthday of the Holy Virgin, the
Mother of God!" That's why he had stopped by the
rowan-tree. I could see he was a holy pilgrim because of
his bag and his boots. I say: "Ivan Fyodorovich, let us go.
Stay with me for as long as you like, I live alone, it's no
trouble for me." I learned later to my surprise that he had
further to go, yet he agreed for my sake to stay.

We talked a lot. I discovered that people must be saved.
When had I had time to think, working at the factory and
raising my son on my own? Later, after my first illness, I
was moved to a desk job for seventy roubles a month, but
all my life I never understood that God is with us. Nobody
understood, especially since they all said God wasn't with
us, and we were supposed to believe we were alone. Life
was hard, there was no time to think, you had to work to
live. Everyone worked and said: "We're alone, there is no

God." And I said it too, because I was young and liked to be the same as the others. But when old people are freed from propaganda they can think as they please, because they don't have to toil away and help society any more. Old people have freedom – Tonya will agree with me there.

Valya looked at Maria. Maria looked at the sea. Maria was thin. Valya gave her a cardigan because it was cold at night, and Maria's chest wheezed. Tonya offered Maria a scarf for her head, but Maria didn't want it. Maria did not know words, she didn't listen to what people said, she just stared at the sea. But she went with them. She slept and ate with them. Whenever she forgot them and went off on her own, they would say to her: "Hey Maria, we've bread for you!" – and she would stay.

Valya had said to Tonya: "Let Maria come with us."

Tonya was frightened that Maria was odd because of the ring on her finger, but nobody came looking for her. Tonya didn't know if it was all right to call her Maria, but Valya said it was. Everyone needs a name, she said, hers can be Maria, and when they reached New Athos the people there could decide what to call her. A pilgrim from Palestine was travelling to New Athos, and this pilgrim would reveal the name Maria. If he couldn't, he would tell them where they should go. Valya knew there were people who could do many things, you just had to find the path to them. Tonya had only recently come and still didn't know anything. Tonya was afraid to talk to Maria because Maria didn't understand, but Valya could see that Maria liked voices. Valya believed that Maria could understand words, but she was scared to tell Tonya. It made Tonya sad that she couldn't talk to Maria, and that Maria wouldn't take her scarf. Tonya worried about being scared of Maria's cold look. Tonya prayed inside herself that Maria would open her mouth and speak her name, that Maria's empty eyes would fill with the warmth of life.

Where two or three are gathered together in my name...

Tonya was still afraid of praying together, for she had only recently come. Valya did not force her. "We'll just whisper inside," she said.

They spread a clean handkerchief on the ground and put out food – bread, three little tomatoes, five potatoes, a jar of pickled red cabbage. Tonya wasn't sure about the red cabbage, and didn't know if you could eat it or not, but Valya said you could. "It's southern cabbage," she said. "At home it's white, here it's red from the sun. You're just not used to it, that's all."

They laid out the food and started making a prayer. They made the prayer with their lips, in case the burning words scorched the newcomer Tonya. The sea was louder than their lips. Maria looked patiently at the sea. She was used to them sighing before eating.

They ate, they watched the dolphins playing and they were happy. Tonya wanted to say the words out loud, to keep saying them. Valya said: "When we say them, He is here."

Tonya was afraid of being seen as she was, and covered her knees with her skirt. This made Valya angry. "It's the toil of your soul He needs," she said, "not how you are on the outside!" But Tonya was shy: the world was beautiful, and Tonya had swollen legs and He would be sad. Tonya knew she knew nothing; the soul wanted to know everything but it wasn't ready, it kept toiling away.

Maria sat on the wet rocks. They should tell her not to sit there. She couldn't live away from the water, that's why they walked along the shore. It hurt their feet to walk by the shore, but if Maria couldn't see the sea she was scared she might run away forever. So Valya opened her knife and sharpened a stick for Tonya, and they all walked along by the sea, Tonya leaning on her stick. Maria walked easily, going far ahead then waiting for their old legs to catch up with her. She would watch them both walking with their sticks and knapsacks, then she would go on. She responded to the name Maria. If they shouted, "Maria, not so fast!", she would sit down and wait.

Their feet were swollen from the hot rocks. There was nobody there. They waded into the water, Maria in her dress, not understanding you had to take it off. The dress was totally bleached in the sun. Maria was black.

Tonya was fearful. She knew she could never keep up with bold Valya. Valya could already swim in the sea. "Come into the water, Maria," she said, "don't just look at it!" So Maria went in and swam with Valya, while Tonya stood in the shallow water by the shore and looked at them in the distance lying silently in the smooth sea.

Tonya loved coolness, gentle sun, slow, simple words. Here the light blazed, and the people above shouted hot, sharp words. The bright sea caressed her weary legs a little. In Athos there were holy places, and that was where they were going. Burned by the sun in her bleached dress, Maria kept walking ahead.

Valya said: "In New Athos there lived learned people. They wrote books. Maybe we'll read there what Maria's name is."

Tonya thought, I've lived my life.

Tonya's husband had been a drunkard. Tonya grew tired of his drinking and fighting, but he would not listen and carried on drinking. Everyone knew he was a drunkard. So Tonya ran away with their little daughter. This drunkard husband got into a fight with his friends who were also drunk, and they smashed in his skull with a hammer. Tonya thought he would die, but they removed the broken bones from his head and put a metal plate there. He came and showed it to her, and she said: "You take the food from your own daughter's mouth – if the doctors had known what you were like, they wouldn't have bothered!" Tonya grabbed her daughter in her arms, and although he shouted he would stop drinking, she banged the door on him forever. Tonya was a beautiful woman and she soon married again. Her new husband was a good man, he worked hard, he never complained and he helped the neighbours. He was often gloomy and tired from working all the time, but at night when they went to bed Tonya would rest her head on the chest of her new husband and hear the firm beat of his tireless heart. Tonya lived the rest of her life with him, and saw her daughter married and her granddaughter born. She lived well.

One day in her old age people came to her and said: "Your drunk husband is dead. Come and say goodbye to him."

At the hospital they pointed to an old, dead man.

"Turn him over," Tonya said.

So they turned him over and she saw the new plate in his mangy old head. "Can't you take it out and give it to someone else?" she asked. But they said they couldn't. Yet again the old drunk had taken everything for himself, leaving nothing for a good person.

They asked her what they should bury him in, and Tonya gave the drunk one of her good husband's suits. "Let him have have it," he said, and the suit and the plate went under the ground.

Then Tonya said to her good husband: "You and I have lived together, you have never offended me. You gave your suit to the drunkard. Now let me roam."

"And will they let me see our granddaughter?" her husband asked.

"Of course they will," said Tonya. "You're her grandfather now."

Then her husband said: "Go Tonya, roam."

And Tonya went.

Tonya wanted to know what life led to, apart from grandchildren, planting trees and good deeds. Where did it lead, what did it aspire to?

Tonya was afraid to think such thoughts, but they wouldn't go away, so she followed on after Valya. Tonya saw big Valya happily splashing in the sea, with the water playing sparks of light over her body. Tonya knew that Valya had three times looked death in the face, and that her own son had gone off cruelly into the unknown and left her. But Valya wasn't afraid of death or of her lost son, she played in the watery element beside silent Maria and laughed, and the light from the waves danced over them.

Tonya looked at the beauty of the world, the un-Russian hills edged with blue smoke, the quiet, laughing sea. Light breezes stroked her, and she thought – can this be? Now? And for every moment of life? Tonya was afraid to bother Him, because before, when she was beautiful like the beauty of the world, she hadn't thought about Him, and now she ran after Him and didn't know whether He could see her or not. He could see Valya of course, Valya lived boldly, she knew the rules, she slept peacefully at night protected by prayer alone, she walked without tiring, and for her there were no obstacles.

Valya led Tonya towards the holy places and said: "Patience. Ask, and it will be given you. Just ask."

Tonya was afraid to wonder what would happen if He wasn't there. But then she remembered the young plate in the dead grey head and she asked shyly: "If possible Lord, please let him enter Thy Kingdom."

His kingdom was blue and high. She didn't know if it was all right to pray for such a drunkard, but Valya led Maria to her and said, "Yes. It's wide open. Let's go."

We found Maria lying by the sea. We bathed her wounds, we removed her scabs and chewed her bread so she could eat it, and she started to live again. Maybe she no longer wanted to live, she just opened and closed her eyes. But we stayed with her all the time, until she finally stood up. How many traces of her past life did she carry with her? Valya healed her and washed her, and we walked on.

"My legs ache," said Tonya.

"Don't walk so fast!" called Valya.

But Maria didn't hear, and ran on ahead.

"Maria, I have some bread here!" Valya called again. "It's right here, our bread!"

Maria turned back lazily and stood a little way off frowning, then sat down to wait.

"I can't walk in the sun any longer," said Tonya and

started to cry.

"Walk along the top, then, through the gardens," said Valya. "We'll push on down here."

"Nothing's right for me," said Tonya. "I'll die in this sun. But walking through the gardens isn't hard enough – it won't count."

Valya shook her head. "No, Tonya. We'd have gone through the gardens too if Maria could have left the sea. We have to go with her because she doesn't know, and we do. We can't abandon her."

"No, we can't," said Tonya, looking at Maria. Maria sat and waited, looking at the sea. Tonya turned from the sea and looked back at the gardens above.

"The monks in New Athos are all dead anyway," said Tonya. "There's other people living there now."

Valya said nothing.

"What I mean is, my strength is gone."

"What about her?" Valya pointed to Maria.

Tonya looked again at Maria. She had no strength left.

"Walk through the gardens," said Valya. "You can come back down with us this evening."

"If we were travelling like normal people we'd have taken the train," said Tonya. "Everything's going dark before my eyes."

"You're right, we'd have taken the train ages ago," agreed Valya.

"If we were young again everything would be fine," said Tonya. "We know, and we'd be young and beautiful in the beauty of the world. But we're not."

"We will be, though," said Valya. "We shall be beautiful in the beauty of the world."

"I won't see it," said Tonya, "I won't see the ancient monks' cypress alley or the monastery in the rock."

Then Valya sat down next to her and started to pray. But Tonya just stretched out and started to die.

Tonya opened her eyes and saw the sky. It was light and quiet. The nearby sea whispered with Valya. Maria dropped a pebble. Smells came down from the gardens.

Down below, life went on. Above was only light, and nobody was there. But Tonya didn't talk about it to Valya, because Valya had a long way to go, leading wretched Maria in the sun. The sun was all around. Somewhere on the other side walked the patient pilgrim from Palestine. Tonya would never see him now. Valya didn't know what to do. Tonya was on the ground dying, and Maria had gone off and wouldn't listen any more. Valya went after Maria and begged her to stay, but Maria went on walking, so Valya prayed harder and turned back towards sad, unmoving Tonya.

She walked. The water lay there. It was bright. The sky watched her walking. Two old women walked after her and brought bread to her. Water and sky, and bread. The old women walked slowly, and she grew angry with them and ran off. The old women lay down. She waited. She was very tired. She was walking so the heavens would move aside for her and no longer stand still, and the water would run beside her. She looked around, but the old women did not get up. She grew alarmed, but the water was shining nearby, and looking at it she forgot everything. She walked and walked. She was hungry, she looked for bread, there was none, nothing but the hot rocks and the birds bobbing in the water watching her. She remembered the old women giving her bread. They weren't there. She looked up at the gardens, the gardens were dark. She walked on without bread.

She grew sleepy and weary of walking. She stumbled against a rock, fell and cut both her knees. They hurt. She stepped into the water. Her legs were pale in the water. Little fish swam up to her knees looking at the blood, and the pain passed. She stood in the water, she lay down in it. There was no bread. She waded out of the water.

It was bright and quiet. The gardens above were heavy. She tugged at her wet dress. A frightened bird cried out, she looked around, it was bright, bright! She stood still. The gardens looked down and were silent. She did not understand and started slowly back, watching the ground beneath her feet. The rocks lay quietly. She walked and watched.

She walked up quietly, they were lying down.

Valya opened her eyes. Tonya didn't open hers.

Valya sat meekly watching her approach.

She came up and sat beside Tonya. The light slowly departed. Valya watched with weak eyes. She sat and watched over Tonya, lying solemnly on the ground. The light departed and died. Valya watched and blinked, her weak, patient eyes looking with their last strength through the dying light.

Maria was troubled by these eyes, she could not look at Valya, she looked at silent Tonya. She lifted Tonya's hand, but the hand resisted and fell back on to the stones.

"Tonya has gone," said Valya.

Maria was troubled. She lay down beside Tonya and turned her back on both of them.

Valya lay down on the other side of Tonya, she didn't want to sit alone and see the light dying.

The light died. A little remained, red in its depths. Above and beyond the gardens something was burning. It was the start of night.

They lay on either side of Tonya, their feet towards the sea and their heads to the gardens. The sea whispered a bit and pulled out, the gardens were silent and shone.

Valya stirred and raised herself up a little. "Maria," she asked shyly, "What is your name?"

"Maria," she spoke.